W9-BNT-032

I've Had a Lot of Fun
The Sodexho Story

I've Had a Lot of Fun

The Sodexho Story

Pierre Bellon
In collaboration with Emily Borgeaud

Sodexho Alliance
Head Office
3, Avenue Newton
78180 Montigny-le-Bretonneux, France
www.sodexho.com

This book is printed on Condat Silk paper,
which is produced according to PEFC monitoring practices regarding the sustainable development
of forests by Condat, an ISO 14001 certified company.

ISBN-13: 978-2-9809575-0-5
ISBN-10: 2-9809575-0-X

Legal Deposit - Bibliothèque et Archives nationales du Québec, 2006
Legal Deposit - Bibliothèque et Archives Canada, 2006

Table of Contents

For convenience, all monetary figures have been converted into 2005 euros.

Introduction

Sodexho is 40 years old.

This is the start of a new chapter in the group's history. With Michel Landel serving as group CEO as of September 1, 2005, a new generation of managers will lead Sodexho into the future. As the group enters a new era, I thought it important to retrace its history, recount its successes and failures, and revisit the philosophy and values upon which its culture is based as well as the major strategic decisions that have driven its development.

The Sodexho Story represents many long months of research and dedication. A team of historians worked closely with the group's communications department, taking inventory of our archives and written materials in order to outline major phases of development and interviewing the group's current

Pierre Bellon
Chairman and Founder, Sodexho

leaders and more than 100 managers who have at least ten years' tenure in various markets. These oral sources were highly valuable, especially in the writing of this book.

I created Sodexho in Marseilles in 1966. As I have said time and time again, "We built Sodexho together." Our group has seen remarkable growth and development over the past 40 years, increasing its revenues by a factor of 11,200 and profits by 7,900, with average annual revenue growth of 27% and average profit growth of 26%. We currently have a presence in 76 countries, employ 325,000 individuals, and enjoy global leadership in most of our client segments.

I would like to thank everyone who helped me build Sodexho, especially the thousands of women and men in the field who, day in and day out, carry out our mission of improving the quality of daily life. Their skill and dedication have always been the driving force behind our ability to satisfy and retain our clients and customers.

I would also like to thank those of Sodexho's managers who played a central role in building our success: Robert Barthélémy, Rémi Baudin, Elisabeth Carpentier, Bernard Carton, Jean-Michel Dhenain, Patrice Douce, Michel Dubois, Raphaël Dubrule, Jean Frégnac, Albert George, Siân Herbert-Jones, Michel Landel, Marie-Pierre Le Lohé and Clodine Pincemin. My thanks also go to all those who have not been mentioned by name.

I would like to thank the members of Sodexho's Board of Directors for their commitment to the group and their skill, honesty and wisdom.

I would like to thank our clients and shareholders for their loyalty.

I would like to thank my grandfather, my mother, who was taken from us too young, and my father. It was by following in their footsteps that my entrepreneurial spirit came to life. And special thanks to my father, who instilled in us his values, raised us and forged a united family.

I would like to thank my sisters Annie and Michèle and my brother Bernard for their trust in me.

Above all, I would like to thank my wife Nani for her affection, intelligence, common sense and endless support; without her, I never would have had the ambition, courage and determination to make Sodexho the group it has become.

Finally, I would like to thank my children Sophie, Nathalie, François-Xavier and Astrid for putting up with my absences and the fact that I never had enough time to show how much I love them. I am deeply proud of their commitment to maintaining Sodexho's independence and longevity.

August 31, 2006

First Era (Beginnings to 1970)

ORIGINS

"Sodexho will be a growth company."

Pierre Bellon, son and grandson of entrepreneurs, made his first foray into the business world in the family shipping supply company in his hometown of Marseilles, after graduating from the leading French business school HEC and serving his military duty in the navy. Bellon was soon convinced that the industry would not survive the massive changes of the 1960s, so he decided to establish a company to deliver meals for companies in the region. His first attempt was far from a roaring success, but it convinced him of one thing: there was room for improvement in the lack-luster options afforded to the increasing numbers of employees eating lunch on the job.

Sodexho was created in 1966 and, in the following year, the Marseilles start-up would cross the Atlantic and become a recognized name in the U.S. within four years.

1

Amidst the Great
Ocean Liners

Clearly, a company's history involves much more than the dreams and abilities of its founder. But while Pierre Bellon has never thought of Sodexho as *his* creation — "A company is more of a team than a person," he often says — Sodexho's beginnings are intimately tied to a young man growing up in Marseilles, in the halcyon years of post-war France. From his roots in the bustling, highly diverse Mediterranean city, his family's ties to the ocean liner and shipping industry, his service in the navy and his passion for travel, Bellon forged a management style, and later a corporate culture, that can be summed up in the expression heard over and over again on Sodexho sites around the world: "I've had a lot of fun."

Old port of Marseilles, France,
beginning of the 20th century

Growing Up in Marseilles

Pierre Bellon was born on January 24, 1930 in Marseilles, France. He spent his childhood and teenage years surrounded by the great ocean liners, steamships and other vessels from around the world that docked there. He was keenly familiar with these ships because they played a central role in his family history.

The Bellons, like many Marseilles families, earned their living from the sea by working in the city's leading industry, the merchant marine. Pierre's grandfather Baptiste-Joseph Bellon (Jean-Baptiste, as he preferred to be called) went on to found the family's company in 1892. Jean-Baptiste yearned to travel the world and saw the navy as his ticket to adventure. But when he was turned away from the navy due to his small stature, he joined Gaymard, supplier to the ocean liners and cargo ships of the Compagnie de Navigation Paquet. He began as a ledger clerk and soon advanced to accountant. Impressed by Jean-Baptiste's entrepreneurial spirit, Frédéric Gaymard approached the young man one day with a unique opportunity: to lead the company's newest venture of supplying the Compagnie de Navigation Mixte. Gaymard told the young man, "It's the opportunity of a lifetime!"

The Bellon shipping supply business was thus created. It would come to employ the next two generations of Bellon men, beginning with Pierre's father, Félix, who joined the company at the age of 18 and assumed its management upon his father's death. Félix's brother Fernand would also join the company, followed by Pierre.

At the end of the 19th century, after seeing its cargo traffic double between 1815 and 1880, Marseilles had become the leading port of France and continental Europe, as well as the center of the French colonial system. Indeed, 90% of the port's activity in the late 1800s was linked to relations with the colonies, of which 75% involved North Africa.

Soon, modern smokestacks began to outnumber the masts of sailboats at dock and envelop them with thick black smoke. The leading Marseilles shipping companies' fleets, often family-owned, played an increasingly major role in the city's development and trade. The plethora of opportunities on land and sea expanded to trade, passenger travel, and shipbuilding and repairs. Among the leading companies were Fraissinet, Fabre, Paquet (the first to offer regular service between Marseilles and Morocco) and the Compagnie de Navigation Mixte.

The family business supplied
the Compagnie de Navigation Mixte

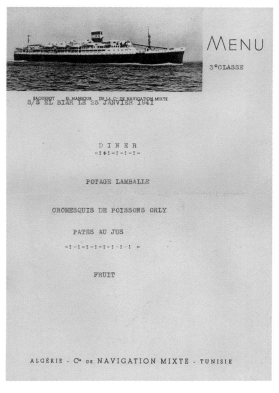

MENU

3° CLASSE

DINER
-:†:-:-:-

POTAGE LAMBALLE

CROMESQUIS DE POISSONS ORLY

PATES AU JUS
-:-:-:-:-:-:-:-:-

FRUIT

ALGÉRIE - C⁰ᵉ DE NAVIGATION MIXTE - TUNISIE

A Compagnie de Navigation
Mixte menu, 1941

Created in 1855, the "Mixte" offered freight and passenger transportation to Algeria and Tunisia and would rank among the leading companies in Marseilles for several decades. It would also earn the reputation of serving the best cuisine on Mediterranean routes, thanks to the services of the Bellon company.

By the time Pierre was growing up, however, Marseilles was quite different from the prosperous city riding the late-19th-century boom in trade and industry. Not only had it suffered from two world wars, but its industrial base was changing, causing a shift in its role as a port city. Increasingly dependent on trade with the colonies, Marseilles also began to serve as a major oil port in the 1930s. The biggest transformations were yet to come, however, and the ocean liner industry, which was so important to the Bellon family's fortunes, was still flourishing.

Despite the proximity of the sea and its ships, Bellon spent most of his time at the Collège de Provence, Marseilles' Jesuit school, which he attended from first through 12th grade. His experiences as a member of the school's Boy Scout troop would have a profound influence on the man he would become. Edouard Richard, leader of Marseilles' 21st troop, the Saint François-Xavier troop, before World War II, recalls, "Pierre was a dedicated, enthusiastic Boy Scout. He was very aware that being a Scout was all about serving others and developing the personality, initiative and team spirit of each troop member."

In 1945, despite a genuine passion for the subject, Bellon failed the philosophy section of the *baccalauréat* examination. He fled the sunshine and temptations of his hometown, exiling himself in Lyons to focus on his studies. Upon passing the scientific section the following June and the philosophy section in September, Bellon told his father that he wanted to attend the prestigious Institute for Political Studies in Paris, in a commitment, he said, "to serving the interests of France." Convinced that his son's character and temperament were not suited to the life of a civil servant, the older Bellon discouraged him, warning him that he would not be happy.

Instead, Pierre decided to apply to HEC, France's leading business school, a more worthy choice for the scion of a successful family of entrepreneurs.

Pierre Bellon as a Boy Scout, 1941

RECOLLECTIONS OF THE COLLÈGE DE PROVENCE

"I remain very attached to my home city of Marseilles, where my wife and I were born, as were our families and children. From first grade through the end of high school, I studied under the tutelage of Jesuit priests at the Collège de Provence. Enrolled at the age of four, I was the youngest and smallest student. My older schoolmates displayed an affection toward me that helped me gain a certain popularity that was not at all unpleasant. Several years later, one of my friends came up with a nickname for me; despite my protests, "Butterball" stuck. When my younger brother Bernard entered the school, he became "Butterball II" and I was rebaptized "Butterball I." This joint moniker only added to our respective notoriety.

"I have wonderful memories of the school's 21st Boy Scout troop. During outings in the hills around Marseilles, we played Catch the Scarf in the scrubland, our calves red and welted from blackberry brambles and nettles, and scrambled down the rocky slopes on the hottest, sunniest days, before diving into the clear, cold water of the rocky inlets below.

"The marvelous memories of my 12 years at the Collège de Provence notwithstanding, I haven't forgotten the Jesuit approach to discipline, as personified by the school's headmaster, Father Moille, a.k.a. "the Whale." Hot-tempered, pudgy and an advocate of tough love, he gave detentions for the smallest, most harmless pranks. However, these disciplinary actions were softened by the passing hours, the clear blue sky at the window, the proximity of the sea and our innate joy at living in Provence."[1]

---

1. Excerpts from Pierre Bellon's testimonial in a book about the Collège de Provence (2000).

The Call to Serve

Pierre Bellon headed to Paris in 1947 to pursue an education at HEC, France's leading business school. After failing the entrance exam three years in a row, he was finally admitted in 1951 and successfully completed the three-year program. "At that time, failing the entrance exam three times was almost unheard of," he admits with a smile. "But I was extremely nervous during the exams and terrible at foreign languages." Once accepted, however, the young man took full advantage of his carefree student years, dividing his time between classes, travel, sports and evenings of bridge, poker and other card games. He also served as vice president of the student body.

At HEC, Pierre met Rémi Baudin, who became a very close friend. They shared many experiences, including working as cruise guides on the *Agamemnon* and taking a bare-bones trip to Yugoslavia in a small truck belonging to the Bellon family. A decade later, after having fallen out of touch, the two friends would cross paths again at Paris' Orly airport, which led to Baudin's joining Sodexho. Today, he serves as vice chairman of Sodexho Alliance's Board of Directors.

Rémi Baudin

A gift from the U.S. government at the end of the war, the destroyer escort F722, *Le Soudanais,* on which Pierre Bellon served his military duty

After graduating from HEC in 1954, Bellon enlisted in the navy for his military service, a natural choice given his curiosity, passion for travel and ongoing connection with the sea. Ensign Bellon would learn a great deal from his journey into the heart of the Suez expedition on the destroyer escort F722, *Le Soudanais.* As for many young men of his generation, his military service kept him on the warship for a long time – 31 months. Fresh out of school, Bellon had managed to make the most of his first occupational experience. Looking back on it, he says, "I learned a great deal from and was very happy to be in the navy." To his credit, Ensign Bellon demonstrated a certain amount of cool-headedness, given the real dangers lurking on the horizon. The experience allowed him to learn many valuable lessons that would serve him well upon creating his own company. Most importantly, he discovered that all men were not created equal, that the strongest men were not necessarily the bravest, and that skilled people did not need to be given orders to get things done.

Learning on the Job

At the end of his military service, Ensign Bellon felt so drawn to the sea that he considered re-enlisting. Less enthusiastic about the idea of becoming a professional navy man, however, the 28-year-old chose instead to join his family's shipping supply company in 1958.

Pierre Bellon began as deputy to the director at Société d'Exploitations Hôtelières Maritimes, Aériennes et Terrestres[1] in 1958 and was promoted to executive vice president the following year. Even though the company had only ten employees, Bellon's immersion in the family business proved to be highly challenging. Just a few months after Pierre joined the family business, his father's right-hand man passed away. Pierre was chosen to assume the responsibilities; he dug out his notes from HEC and delved into the task of learning how to manage a small company.

In fact, the Bellon business was a federation of small companies, all involved in shipping supply, which Félix and Fernand had created after taking over the business when their father died. One example was Société Méditerranéenne d'Approvisionnements Généraux (SOMAG), which was set up in 1945. It not only supplied Société d'Exploitations Hôtelières

1. In 1955, brothers Félix and Fernand divided up the family assets. Fernand took control of Promar, an anchovy factory that had been created in the late 1930s, and Félix consolidated the family's shipping supply business through the creation of the Société d'Exploitations Hôtelières Maritimes, Aériennes et Terrestres.

"Trying to shape economic forces to serve mankind."

Maritimes, Aériennes et Terrestres, whose sole customer was Compagnie de Navigation Mixte, it also supplied other ships from around the world that put in at Marseilles. Additionally, the Bellon family had acquired stakes in four small shipping supply companies that dealt in non-food items.

Another member company was Société Générale de Ravitaillement (SGR), which was created in Algeria by Pierre's father and two other families in 1958, the same year Pierre joined the family business. It supplied French companies operating in the Sahara Desert oilfields following the discovery of the first oil and natural gas fields deep underground, 30 years after the prophecies of Conrad Kilian. Campsites blossomed in the desert around the oil wells, bringing with them entire encampments of people who needed to be housed and fed. With the boom came a need for new roads, buildings and other infrastructure. Investments in the Sahara oil business between 1952 and 1962 reached some 1.1 billion euros, of which 30% was spent on transportation and services alone. There were tremendous opportunities for those brave enough to accompany the developers of the Sahara oil fields. Under the leadership of Pierre Bellon and two other managers, SGR attained success, but could not survive the Algerian independence movement. However,

Bellon would discover through this experience the remote-site business that would later write a decisive chapter in Sodexho's history.

During this period, Pierre was also learning his craft as a manager and entrepreneur, both on the job and by meeting other business leaders in the community. In 1958, a friend suggested that he join the Centre des Jeunes Patrons (CJP, Young Business Leaders' Association), an organization of young employers united in the belief that companies should serve the good of mankind. The CJP was a small, dynamic organization that was stirring up the more established CNPF (National Association of French Business Leaders). To his surprise, Bellon found that the CJP was anything but a waste of his time; rather, he found its debates and discussions to be extremely valuable. "I learned so much from the CJP. Most importantly, I realized that we should work to make economic forces serve mankind, a philosophy compatible with my Christian education."

"Upon attending my first workshop, I felt very flattered that the leader of the group was actually interested in what I had to say," recalls Bellon. "He was responsible for managing 1,500 employees, whereas my staff numbered about ten. I often wonder if my desire to run a large company was born from that

Pierre Bellon during
a presentation at the Young
Managers' Association, 1969

"Sodexho would never have become what it is today had it not been for the CJD's influence on Pierre Bellon."

experience. The following year, we addressed the subject, 'Strengths and Weaknesses of Family Businesses.' All participants were free to speak about their difficulties, including those they would never dare mention to father or uncle. Very few of us had managed to successfully reconcile the roles of family member, manager and shareholder, which is something that often prevented family-owned companies from functioning or advancing as they should have. Thanks to these discussions, I was later able to gather the courage and determination to tell my father that I wanted to start my own organization."

Pierre Bellon served as president of the CJP Marseilles from 1963 to 1964 and subsequently led the national group from 1968 to 1970, during which time he succeeded in renaming the organization the CJD (Centre des Jeunes Dirigeants, or Young Managers' Association). The shift from *patron* (owner) to *dirigeant* (manager) reflected a more accessible, democratic philosophy.

Bellon was also greatly influenced by his participation in a committee responsible for engaging managers, executives and union representatives in constructive social dialogue. "It was an unforgettable experience," recalls Bellon. "Having grown up in a well-to-do community, I had preconceived notions of certain social classes." A compassionate manager, he would place importance on discussions between unions and management, dedicating time to them and using them as a catalyst to find solutions for improving work conditions, increasing salaries, providing employee training and improving the reputation of an under-appreciated profession.

An active observer of and actor in the local community, Bellon soon came to realize that the Marseilles shipping supply industry's days were numbered. Following the decolonization movement, the major shipping companies had seen a decrease in activity by the early 1960s. More importantly, they were threatened by the rapid growth of air travel. The demise of the shipping industry was imminent. In 1958, France's domestic airline Air Inter celebrated its inaugural flight and the number of passengers passing through the Marseilles-Marignane airport increased more than tenfold in 14 years, from 35,000 in 1938 to 370,000 in 1952, eventually reaching 930,000 in 1959.

"I understood how important people and their individual actions are to a company's success."

Some shipping lines that specialized in passenger transportation entered the air travel market at this time. However, only a few companies would be able to survive an industry shake-up in the 1960s. The Compagnie de Navigation Mixte would suffer a sad fate: it would find itself in the late 1960s without a single ship under its name for the first time.

Humble Beginnings

As Bellon's concern about the future of the industry grew, he began to consider evolving the family business. At the headquarters of the Bellon family, Place de La Joliette, in Marseilles' shipping district, passionate discussions were the order of the day.

SHRM (Société Hôtelière et de Ravitaillement Maritime), a powerful international financial group and competitor of the Bellon family, had launched Télérestor, which delivered meals to corporate clients from a self-service cafeteria in downtown Marseilles. Always on the lookout for new opportunities, Bellon followed the Télérestor initiative closely. When he saw that Télérestor was already serving 1,000 meals per day, he began to think seriously of giving it a go himself.

In 1962, Bellon launched Repas Service out of his Uncle Fernand's anchovy factory's warehouse. Pierre invested in an oven, containers and a small truck. He hired a handful of employees to prepare and deliver meals to companies in the metropolitan Marseilles area. In 1963, he hired Robert Barthélémy, a young Marseilles native and HEC graduate, to develop the business further.

Pierre Bellon
at the port of Marseilles

This undertaking proved to be a major challenge. The two young men soon realized there was a huge gap between supplying luxury liners, where meals were prepared on board, and delivering ready-to-eat meals to corporate clients. One of the first Sodexho brochures highlighted Sodexho's unique approach: "The company began by combining two industries that seemed incompatible. Its ambitious plan was to couple the skills and respect for French culinary traditions with the Bellon family's quality service, developed through 60 years in the shipping supply business, to benefit the growing number of men and women whose professional obligations required them to eat and sometimes even sleep away from their homes."

Back then, the main problem was keeping meals hot until they could be served. Despite the use of insulated containers and efforts to shorten delivery times, the meat dishes and french fries would inevitably arrive

THE FIRST CANTEEN

According to some sources, the Banque de France was the first French company to offer its employees a canteen in 1866. In 1913, it would also be the first to subcontract its cafeteria's operations to a private company. This represented a break with tradition, because these services were typically managed by the companies and schools where the cafeterias were located. That same year, French legislation required a dining area with a fresh-water fountain in every company where 25 or more employees wished to eat their meals on-site.

In 1945, the role of the staff cafeteria was reaffirmed by a ruling that instituted a workers' council in every company. Difficulties arose in the 1950s as the cafeterias, often operated by company employees or the workers' council, grew rapidly, some serving as many as 20,000 meals per day. To ward off inevitable "sandwich strikes," companies increasingly hired specialists in the field. This led to rapid expansion of the food services sector in the 1960s and 1970s.

at the client site overcooked and soggy. Food that was initially high-quality wound up lackluster on the customer's plate, due to Marseilles' traffic conditions and inadequate delivery equipment. "We were delighted to be serving 350 meals per day in the face of serious competition," recalls Bellon, "but we were losing clients as quickly as we were gaining them."

Although Repas Service was not the rousing success he had hoped it would be, Bellon was convinced that corporate food services had great potential. He contemplated approaching the market differently by preparing meals at client sites and by offering higher quality services.

During this launch of modern-day food services, leading companies were assessing the market, including the powerful SHRM group. This company had built a shipping supply empire after its founding in 1902 under the name Calizi et Nivière, managing the ships of four organizations: the Compagnie des Transports Océaniques, the Société Maritime d'Extrême-Orient, the Compagnie des Messageries Maritimes, and the Compagnie Générale Transatlantique. The fleets of the latter two companies comprised nearly 80 vessels, whereas the Mixte counted only 15. SHRM also operated the Tan Son Nhut airfield in Vietnam in 1946 and was active in the Sahara Desert in the early 1950s, supplying provisions and beverages to oil companies and operating their bases, including in Hassi Messaoud, Algeria. In 1963, the successful Télérestor venture that was launched the previous year paved the way for the creation of SHR (Société Hôtelière de Restauration), a subsidiary of the group dedicated to providing "mass food services to companies" in France.

"By the early 1960s, the decolonization movement in Africa, the end of the company's passenger liner monopoly to Algeria, and the demise of liner services to the Far East led SHRM to explore new markets," where, according to a company brochure, "its SHR subsidiary could offer food services for companies and organizations of all kinds." As it expanded, SHR could draw on its parent's deep financial resources and international network, which made even the most daring competitors think twice before entering the market. Bellon, however, rose to the challenge of catching up to and ultimately surpassing the giant company.

Another formidable competitor was Jacques Borel, who had founded Société Générale de Restauration in 1959 and created Wimpy, France's first fast-food chain, in 1961. He was so successful that at one point Bellon had considered joining forces with him in the Provence region.

Jean Frégnac

A few months before creating Repas Service, Bellon met Jean Frégnac, whom he would later refer to as his professional mentor. At the time, Frégnac was a consultant specializing in small companies at the first French consulting firm, Paul Planus. Frégnac worked regularly for a variety of Marseilles companies and the city's Chamber of Commerce. "I had been in Marseilles for three to four years and was friends with many of Pierre Bellon's acquaintances," he recalls. "It wasn't as if I were on unfamiliar ground or a consultant coming from Paris. Pierre told me that he needed some advice and things quickly fell into place." The two men established a highly trusting relationship and, over the years, Frégnac would provide important insights in helping to develop Bellon's ideas, leveraging lessons learned with other clients, especially family-owned companies.

With the ideas, actors, marketplace and competitive landscape defined and in place, the stage was now nearly ready for Bellon's vision of Sodexho to take flight. All that was missing was a stroke of magic that only the most creative entrepreneur could bring about. But even this last touch would never have been enough if it were not for the audacity of the young Bellon.

2

Dare to Win

Two years after creating Repas Service, while still administering the family enterprise, Pierre Bellon began to consider the possibility of starting his own company. As it turned out, a conversation at a college alumni meeting was all that it took to provide the spark that launched the adventure.

Initial Victories

On a balmy summer evening in 1964, HEC alumni in Marseilles held one of their frequent reunions, this time aboard a yacht. In the middle of a conversation, someone from SHRM happened to mention that the company was bidding to operate the new cafeteria at the Atomic Energy Commission (CEA) Pierrelatte site, located in the Drôme (Provence). "The contract is worth a fortune," he added. Bellon and Robert

"We built Sodexho one brick at a time."

Barthélémy looked at each other without saying a word. As they left together, just a few minutes of discussion was all they needed to make up their minds.

The following morning, the two men showed up at the CEA in Pierrelatte, where the head of the purchasing department and project manager informed them that the tender was closed. Bellon and Barthélémy managed to persuade him to extend the deadline by two weeks in order to give them time to develop an offer.

Thus began a race against time – and a major challenge. Not only were the two men facing competition from the far better resourced SHRM and Jacques Borel, but it was the first time they had ever bid on such a large project. "We took a huge risk," Bellon admitted later. "Jumping in like that, offering service for 2,000 employees in a brand new cafeteria. If we kept people waiting two hours for lunch on the first day, we knew there'd be hell to pay." What's more, their lack of experience or major contracts in corporate food services meant that Bellon and Barthélémy had to find another way to inspire confidence in the decision-makers at the CEA. The only solution was to innovate. "I couldn't help feeling intimidated by our competitors," Bellon recalls. "They were major players already established in the sector. I knew that we had very little credibility and that the

CEA in Pierrelatte would require us to offer competitive prices. There was only one possible solution: we would have to offer something no one else had ever thought of."

The company drew on all of its existing resources for the bid, and to gain valuable insider knowledge, Robert Barthélémy participated in a ten-day food services internship at one of the biggest companies in the region, Sud Aviation in Marignane, which operated its own highly regarded cafeteria. The experience enabled him to see how things were done and to calculate how many staff members would be needed at Pierrelatte. With this new knowledge in hand, Bellon submitted an offer to the CEA that emphasized transparency and client service as the foundation for the business relationship. To address concerns about his company's lack of experience, he responded that his team had been present on-site throughout the entire bidding process, whereas his competitors had gone on vacation. He also guaranteed the level of quality and a high degree of transparency. If awarded the contract, his company would report its expenditures and revenues to the CEA on a monthly basis, he explained. Most importantly, he would have his managers trained

"We would have to offer something no one else had ever thought of."

at the cafeteria of Sud Aviation and would put the management team in place six weeks before opening the CEA cafeteria.

The CEA in Pierrelatte could not help but be impressed, and they accepted Bellon's bid, to the discontent and disbelief of the competition. However, Bellon was told that he would have to offer the same prices imposed by the CEA on all bidders. Realizing that it would be very difficult to guarantee the promised level of quality at that price, Bellon hesitated. He realized he would lose money on the deal, but he also knew that such an opportunity would not come twice. He signed the contract and assembled a 70-member team for the CEA site, but not without warning his client that, given its anticipated monthly losses, his company would go bankrupt within six months.

A few months later, after suffering a 10% loss in revenues, Bellon asked the CEA in Pierrelatte for a price increase of a few cents per meal. The CEA had been very pleased with its selection, because employees were delighted with the new cafeteria and its high-quality services. Bolstered by the fact that he had informed his client in writing that his company was going to lose money by providing services at the agreed-upon price, Bellon finally turned to the CEA's headquarters management team in Paris. Negotiations

THE ROLE OF A SITE MANAGER

"I'd get up very early and head to the market to buy fruit and vegetables," recalls Etienne Dadaglio. "Dairy products were delivered by the reps who came to see us. The butcher was the only supplier who didn't deliver product.

"It was up to the most resourceful people to negotiate with their suppliers. Learning on the job in that way was a fascinating, rewarding experience. I also understood how important it was to be very disciplined about managing each penny. I came from the traditional restaurant business, so this was something new to me. Once the shopping was done, I'd get to work with the kitchen team. Thanks to the implementation of a system that allowed us to price each item on the menu separately rather than fixing a set price for a full meal, we enjoyed a certain liberty in creating dishes and menus.

Compared to modern-day kitchens, ours were not very advanced, but they were still an improvement on the previous generation of mess halls, with their big pots of food for six to eight people.

"In the afternoons, I'd dedicate my energies to managing our company. At that time, we had not yet created the innovative ways to assess daily food costs that Sodexho is known for today. We listed all of the items in our inventory on the same large documents used aboard ships and managed our details following navy rules. As a matter of fact, most of our managers were former ship stewards and I was an exception. We called our headquarters in La Joliette every night to report production costs, which were calculated based on our sales and expenditures."

were tough, but Bellon finally got what he was asking for. He gently teased his client that, "'Given your level of responsibility, surely the hour you just spent with me is worth the modest annual increase that I am asking for.' But I said it so nicely that they had to laugh and we managed to work things out," recalls Bellon. From then on, any decisions regarding the price of meals were made separately by each site rather than by the CEA headquarters in Paris.

Bellon's daring and innovative approach paid off. Shortly after winning the CEA contract, he signed on other clients in the Marseilles area, including a ship-building company (700 meals a day) and the CEA site in Marcoule (1,500 meals a day). He realized that he had to move quickly, for these initial successes were proving that the sector did indeed have a future.

Ready, Set, Go!

"Like our father before him, Pierre is a family leader and the head of the Bellon family tribe," says Pierre's sister Michèle. "Since we are from the south of France, that is the way we like it." Bellon felt as strongly about building a successful company as he did about his position as leader of his clan. When he created Sodexho on March 9, 1966, he made sure that the company was structured in a way that would allow him to manage it under optimal conditions while still maintaining a united family. Thanks to the CJD and Jean Frégnac's advice, he was attuned to the potential dangers facing a family-run business. He honored his father's request that his brother and sisters participate in the capital of Sodexho, using a family charter to outline their roles and define their conditions. Pierre would control and hold the majority of capital, and his brother and sisters would be shareholders only, unable to interfere in the management of the company. The family agreement also required him to set a minimum level of dividends to be paid to family shareholders. If he failed to meet these conditions, his brother and sisters would be entitled to sell their shares back to him at a price determined by a third-party expert. However, if the conditions were met – as would be the case throughout Sodexho's history – the shareholders would not have the right to intervene in the management of the company. To this day, 40 years later, this principle of "separating family and business issues" remains a fundamental rule.

While Pierre was creating Sodexho, his father, Felix Bellon, had placed the various family companies under a holding company he ran, Felix Bellon SA, which included the family's interests in the shipping

Jacques Tavel

Pierre Sannini

Michel Lorin

supply sector and its foodstuff supply activity via SOMAG. It also included the shipping and industrial supply company AMI, and SGR, which continued to carry out activities in Algeria.

It proved to be an exciting period, filled with new ideas and initiatives. Things started happening quickly. Rémi Baudin joined the company in 1965, followed by Jacques Tavel and Pierre Sannini in 1966. Michel Lorin also figured among the ranks of Sodexho recruits who would spearhead new activities and create the supporting organization.

Everyone functioned somewhat as a one-man band, similar to the multiple roles of a site manager acting simultaneously as chef, buyer and trainer. "Everyone supported everyone else, regardless of formal roles," recalls Sannini, who joined Sodexho as an assistant in the accounting department. "If the receptionist was out, someone else would pick up the phone when it rang. If the person who handled payroll was on vacation, a couple of people would take on the job."

Sodexho's early pioneers were enthusiastic, daring multi-taskers who shared a genuine dedication toward their clients. They had everything to gain by working in a sector that was still in its infancy.

BETWEEN PARIS AND ATHENS

Traveling companions during their HEC days, Pierre Bellon and Rémi Baudin had lost touch with one another. They met up again in 1965 by chance. Baudin was standing in line at Orly Airport in Paris waiting to check in for a flight to Athens when he ran into Bellon, who was headed to the Middle East via Athens. On the same plane for the first leg of the trip, the two men had plenty of time to catch up. Baudin was working for a French consulting firm in Athens but was considering leaving the consulting field to take on a more operational position. Bellon shared his growing conviction that the food services sector had a bright future. Two weeks later, Baudin received a letter from Bellon. It read, "I told you about my current project. I think you're the perfect person to run our shipping supply business, which would allow me to focus on food services. I'm ready to hire you whenever you want." And that's exactly what happened…a few months later, Baudin came aboard.

"It was a fascinating experience," says Tavel, who, upon being hired to create a design department in Marseilles, learned to draw at the city's Ecole d'Architecture. "We were the pioneers of the modern-day food services industry. We were transforming ordinary cafeterias into inviting, appealing dining areas. It was hard work. Our value-added services were unique compared to those offered by our competitors, because we were establishing true partnerships with our clients and helping them beyond their basic, immediate needs."

From its first year of business, the new team enjoyed great success in Sodexho's chosen territory of southeastern France, as well as in southwestern France, the Rhône-Alps region and the Paris area. Sodexho's first regional headquarters was set up in Pau, in the Pyrénées, where the company signed two contracts totaling 1,200 meals per day with oil company SNPA, the forerunner of Elf-Aquitaine. Sodexho's second regional headquarters would be set up under the direction of Michel Lorin in Grenoble. He had already worked a quick stint at Cogolin's vacation camp, where attempts to penetrate the leisure sector had proved unsuccessful. The Grenoble site's first client was the Péchiney research center in Voreppe. "We had to improvise when the cafeteria first opened on August 16, 1966, as we were still waiting for the final structure to be completed," recalls Michel Lorin. "I had never hired anyone before, and suddenly I had to hire a site manager. We began at 50 meals a day, but after the cafeteria was completed, the number of meals soared to 250. I suffered many sleepless nights before the opening, because it was a true beginning in so many ways. Everything was up in the air."

"My enthusiasm for the food services sector soared," he adds. "Lunchtime represented a pleasant moment in the lives of the people we were serving. The food was good and they were happy with our services. We also enjoyed stellar growth, signing 12 contracts in Grenoble in just over one year. We managed to build our market share, even in the face of competition from the Compagnie des Wagons-Lits, Jacques Borel and SHR."

Everyone had more than enough work to keep themselves busy, when an event led Bellon and the Sodexho team to turn their attention to a distant land 9,000 km from Paris, between the Atlantic Ocean and the immense Amazon forest.

A Remote French Territory

The 700 inhabitants of the small village of Kourou, French Guiana were about to embark on an adventure with space exploration that would change the course of their destiny.

Determined to catch up with the United States and the Soviet Union – which had launched the first space research artificial satellite, *Sputnik*, in 1957 – Europe was busy creating its first space research institutions in the early 1960s. One of the major players in the European space exploration movement was the French CNES (National Center for Spatial Studies), which was responsible for such accomplishments as the 1965 launch of the *Diamant A* rocket out of Hammaguir, Algeria, an event that made France the world's third space power.

Following Algeria's independence, France needed to find a new location for its space program. After much deliberation, the French government decided in April 1964 to build a new CNES launch site in Kourou, French Guiana.

Sodexho might never have sought opportunities in French Guiana had it not been for Bellon's interest in the emerging field of space exploration. A particular commercial opportunity also contributed to the company's pursuit of business in South America. In 1966, the CNES began to search for someone to handle food services on its construction site in Kourou. Sodexho joined the candidate pool, despite the fact that it would require a considerable investment from the young company. Unfortunately, SHRM won the bid. Reflecting on this, Bellon says, "We had been beaten, but I stuck to my guns. I went to see General Aubinière, CNES president and founder of the Concorde airplane program. I asked, 'General, why didn't you pick Sodexho?' He replied, 'It was a difficult decision. We like your company and the fact that it is very small, but your competitors went to French Guiana to prepare the bid, whereas you did not.' He urged me not to become discouraged and to keep up the good work. He told me, 'We will begin another bid process for a second service provider in Kourou,

André Langlois

because we need someone to manage a range of services including housekeeping and gardening.' I told him we had no experience in that area and would not be able to participate. We had spent too much money on the first bid and could not afford a second failure. 'Mr. Bellon,' he replied, 'you should come up with an offer. I appreciate the fact that your company looked at our needs in great detail and I believe that you really understand the constraints and expectations of the CNES. I also know that you believe in the future of the Kourou site. There are not many companies that will be interested in this bid or in French Guiana. You must go there and participate in the bid. If you come up with a competitive offer, I will give you the contract.'"

And so it was. After signing its first contract with the CNES in 1967, Sodexho set up a team at the French Guiana construction site that same year. The launch site and most of the technical buildings would be ready in 1968. Once again, Lady Luck had dealt a very good hand to Bellon. Upon asking Colonel André Langlois to help him prepare Sodexho's second bid to the CNES, Bellon discovered that the Colonel was quite familiar with the French Guiana territory. After a few months of reintegration into the civilian world at Sodexho, Colonel Langlois was hired at the

Sodexho's French Guiana brochure, 1968

beginning of the second bid process. Thanks to his participation, the company submitted a thorough bid and won the contract.

Sodexho's responsibilities evolved with the development and changing needs of the CSG (Guiana Space Center) to include the maintenance of the roads and sites of the *Diamant* rocket and other rocket probes; grounds-keeping in Kourou; fire safety procedures and equipment; and the construction and management of a hotel and small supermarket.

"For me and for those who had been with Sodexho from the very beginning, our success was unbelievable. In some ways, we had actually grown up with the company."

As Sodexho entered new fields, it confronted and overcame a diversity of challenges that would help the company to become a pioneer in offering multiple services. Where the company lacked certain skills, it sought experts in that field to answer the needs of its clients. For example, Sodexho worked with Paris firemen to conceive and implement Kourou's fire safety system. The company was also responsible for the construction and opening of a small supermarket, whose operations it managed until other stores were opened in the new city of Kourou in 1971. When the CNES asked him to finance the supermarket, Bellon did not hesitate and turned to the Bank of French Guiana. "The CNES is asking me to finance this supermarket," he explained, "but I don't have the funds." He then described the contract on which Sodexho was bidding. "Mr. Bellon," replied his contact at the bank, "it's simple. If you win the contract, we'll fully finance the project."

As a prestigious client reference, the CNES contract played a key role in getting Sodexho off the ground and then driving the young company's expansion in France and the rest of Western Europe. Without the CNES and the CEA, Bellon would later concede, Sodexho would never have risen to become the company that it is today.

Adventures in Brazil

After slightly more than a year of working in French Guiana, Sodexho was presented with an opportunity in 1968 to cross the border into Brazil. Forex, for whom Sodexho operated an oil rig in the Bay of Biscay, had just signed a contract with Petrobras to build an oil rig off the shore of Maceió in northeastern Brazil; they wanted Sodexho to provide certain services on the new rig. Interested in exploring opportunities in the Americas beyond French Guiana, Pierre Bellon was won over when he visited Rio and the beaches of Copacabana for the first time.

Sodexho headed to Brazil first to settle the oil rig's kitchen and accommodation equipment needs. After the contract was secured in 1968 by Rémi Baudin, it was handed over to Michel Lorin, whose mission in Rio was twofold: he would manage operations on the oil rig, and he would seek new clients in the food services sector. Although he did not know a soul in Rio, he located many companies that were interested in food services. Despite the promising reports he sent to Bellon, however, the contracts were slow in coming and the latter began to wonder if there was indeed a market for food services in Brazil, where companies rarely offered food services onsite. Instead,

Sodexho's first sales brochure, 1967

"Company restaurants are not canteens any more. They embody a social purpose that aims to increase employees' productivity and improve the working experience."

employees would lunch on sandwiches that they brought to work. At the end of 1969, Bellon decided that the market in Brazil was not ready for Sodexho. It took him an hour on the phone to convince Michel Lorin to come home, as the latter was reluctant to abandon the opportunities he saw were possible.

"Sodexho has a presence in French Guiana and Brazil," Bellon argued. "It would be a strategic error to develop our activities in Brazil before conquering Lyons and Paris. We must continue to develop our business in the French market." Sodexho's short foray into Brazil did serve a purpose, however. The company was able to reduce supply costs for its contracts in Kourou by importing high quality meat directly from Brazil.

Once it had defined France as its priority, Sodexho pursued a strategy to steadily dominate that market, first developing its client base in Marseilles, Pau, Grenoble, Toulouse and Lyons, and then gaining ground in Paris. The company worked slowly and steadily, without drawing much attention to itself, contrary to competitor Jacques Borel, who made sure he appeared in the papers regularly.

3

The Little Enterprise
That Could

In the four years following Sodexho's creation, the Board of Directors' reports all seemed to start the same way: "Sodexho continued to expand quickly in 1967… 1968… 1969… 1970." In just four years, Sodexho had spread like wildfire, surpassing the symbolic milestone of 1,000 employees in 1969. At the end of that year, the company was serving 31,000 meals at 62 sites. In accordance with its founder's philosophy, Sodexho had been a "growth company" since its creation. Yet, had it not been for a deeply-rooted commitment to the company's mission and values from the very beginning, Sodexho surely would not have succeeded when facing the numerous challenges of growing the company from 300 to more than 1,500 employees.

"Pierre Bellon imagined Sodexho before he created it."

1966–1970: Sodexho's Growth

1966	1967	1968	1969	1970
Revenues in millions of euros				
1.0	1.5	2.1	5.9	8.9
Net income in euros				
25,000	81,500	173,000	168,700	197,300
Number of employees				
312	530	762	1,082	1,642
Number of dining facilities				
13	26	42	62	113

During this exuberant period of growth and development, each employee was responsible for shaping his or her own role, and company policies evolved as needed. At the same time, Pierre Bellon's project was slowly taking shape, as were the major guiding principles that would remain in place 40 years later.

"What's a Company for?"

Very few entrepreneurs wrestle with the philosophical issue of their company's larger purpose in the world. Instead, their stories are more often told from the glamorous perspective of a revolutionary innovation or a fantastically successful product. But while Bellon was obviously attuned to the market and the business, his vision was shaped by a far broader yet highly pragmatic exploration of a company's larger role. This was also reflected in his regular involvement in organizations like the Economic and Social Council and the National Association of French Business Leaders, now known as the MEDEF.

Basically, Bellon formed his company in his mind before actually incorporating it. "In 1965," recalls Jean Frégnac, "before Sodexho was even created, Bellon had me write down the company's philosophy, mission and general goals, in exactly the same terms as you see today."

"During the 1960s in France, Marxist philosophy was still in vogue and many questioned the notion of private enterprise," reflects Bellon. "That's why, before creating Sodexho, I asked myself why I wanted to start a company. The answers I came up with then remain the basis for Sodexho's philosophy: a company is a community of clients, customers, employees and shareholders. I told myself that I wanted to build a company that would meet the expectations of these three groups, expectations that can be contradictory, at least in the short term. The only way to do this is through organic growth. That's why, even before founding the company, I decided that Sodexho would be a growth company.

"I was terrified by the possibility of a recession, after having witnessed the demise of shipyards and ship repair companies in Marseilles and its surroundings. Thousands of people had been laid off. I told myself that it would be catastrophic if I ever had to fire people."

Pierre Bellon

"I made organic growth a priority from the start."

SODEXHO'S PHILOSOPHY

Prior to founding Sodexho, Pierre Bellon asked himself, "What is the purpose of creating your own company?" His answers at that time formed and still form the basis of our corporate philosophy.

Who we are

Our company is a community of our clients, customers, employees and shareholders. Our purpose is to exceed their expectations.

Our business strategy: organic growth

We continue to focus on achieving organic growth in earnings and revenues, while contributing to the economic development of the countries in which we operate.

Our mission

To create and offer services that contribute to a more pleasant way of life for people, wherever and whenever they come together. To "Improve the Quality of Daily Life."

Our goal

To be recognized by our clients as the benchmark wherever we offer our services, in every country, in every region, in every locale.

Our core values

Service spirit

More than 97% of our employees are in direct day-to-day contact onsite with clients and customers. This demands exceptional human qualities and specific behavior that we call service spirit.

Clients and customers are at the center of everything we do.

To serve them well each day and at all levels, we must demonstrate our availability, our ability to listen, our capacity to anticipate their expectations, our sense of conviviality, our responsiveness to their remarks and our pride in satisfying them.

Sodexho has become a large, worldwide company, yet we remain a local company where each manager in the field is a true entrepreneur, close to the client and empowered to make decisions.

Team spirit

A winning team is one whose members demonstrate respect and appreciation for each other.

It is an absolute need in all of our operations, business units and administrative offices, as well as in our management committees.

Each person's skills combine with other team members' knowledge to help ensure Sodexho's success. Teamwork depends on the following: listening, transparency, respect for others, diversity, solidarity in implementing major decisions, respect for rules and mutual support, particularly in difficult times.

Spirit of progress

Our team members strive to give their best and continuously improve our performance. This spirit of progress makes itself known through:

- Our will, but also the firm belief that one can always improve the current situation.
- Acceptance of the evaluation of one's performance and comparison with colleagues in the company or with competitors.
- Our accountability for our actions, our spirit to move forward and our refusal to have a culture of blame.
- Self-criticism, because understanding one's successes as well as one's failures is fundamental to continuous improvement.
- A balance between ambition and humility.
- Optimism, the belief that for every problem there is a solution, an innovation, or some way to progress.

Our ethical principles (formed in 2003)

Trust

Trust is one of the cornerstones of our operations. It is a foundation of loyalty between Sodexho and its clients, employees and shareholders that is based on honest, open relations.

Respect for people

People are at the heart of our business.

Sodexho is committed to providing equal opportunities regardless of race, origin, age, gender, beliefs, religion, physical ability or sexual orientation.

Improving quality of life means according each person respect, dignity and consideration.

Transparency

This is one of Sodexho's major principles and an important part of our culture. We are committed to continuous transparency with all stakeholders: clients, customers, employees and shareholders.

Business integrity

We do not tolerate any practice that is not born of honesty, integrity and fairness, anywhere we do business.

We clearly communicate our position on this issue to our clients, suppliers and employees, and expect them to share our rejection of unethical, illegal and unfair practices.

"Today it's easy to talk about company policies, but at that time, we were defining them on a daily basis."

From the very beginning, each employee carried a card stating the company's purpose, values and mission. While this technique may seem banal to some, it was anything but common practice for a small French company at the end of the 1960s.

Shaping a New Profession

At a time when companies in the service industry were like "third-class citizens of the business world," according to Bellon, Sodexho's sales approach centered on the premise that the client was king. "In my heart of hearts, I believed that the food services market of the 1960s held great opportunity. I wasn't completely sure of myself, however, and had doubts about getting started. At the time, some companies in France were being crippled by 'sandwich strikes' that employees instigated to protest the quality of lunches served. The sector had a very bad image and quality was at rock bottom. I decided to take a chance, but would base my actions on a very clear philosophy. I was determined to improve the quality of the meals served on company premises."

And Bellon managed to do just that. In 1969, this headline appeared in the company's brochure: "You won't find Sodexho in any restaurant guides . . . but that's only because they don't list cafeterias yet."

"From the very beginning," says Bellon, "we were obsessed with improving quality. But to develop our activities, we also looked at increasing sales per client by offering the widest range of food services possible, and a comprehensive range of non-food-related services."

Despite limited financial resources, Sodexho devised a customized offering and stayed close to its clients. District managers were always located within two hours of the sites they oversaw so they could quickly respond if needed, and regional headquarters were given complete authority to resolve issues within their geographical zone.

Some may argue that it was neither remarkable nor particularly innovative to offer customized solutions in a market where each client has specific needs. But Bellon was able to transform the constraints of the food services sector into differentiating factors for his company that enabled it to beat the competition.

The company's human resources policies also supported this unique culture and way of working. In a business serving a wide range of clients on sites around the world, site managers obviously have to

Sodexho brochure cover, 1969

"You won't find Sodexho in any restaurant guides ... but that's only because they don't list cafeterias yet."

Extract:
"Employee needs differ from one company to another, according to the company itself, its sector of activity, its way of getting things done, and the culture of the region where it is located. Sodexho's ability to adapt to different conditions enables it to meet all these needs. Our goal is to provide the highest level of service, not by imposing a standardized solution, but by adapting each solution to the working conditions of each company."

"Without the professionalism and dedication of our cafeteria personnel in France when the company was in its infancy, our organization would never have developed the way it did. Word-of-mouth was critical to building a stellar business and our reputation at that time."

have the initiative and authority to run their own operations. This characteristic would become a source of pride and one of the hallmarks of a company that described itself as a "federation of entrepreneurs," a reflection of the pioneering spirit of its founders.

Proper financial guidelines were a key element of Sodexho's model for success from the outset. "A company that doesn't grow will not survive, but a company that grows too rapidly without respecting certain financial principles will go bankrupt," says Bellon. "I was faced with the problem of growing a company with small financial resources. I wanted to maintain our independence in order to safeguard our values and strategy, and to meet our employees' expectations. I was extremely wary of banks and other financial institutions and decided early on that we had to ask clients in the food services sector to invest in their own premises. I resolved that our company's level of capital intensity should be very low . . . I also realized that we should not spend more than we earned and did everything I could to ensure that our clients paid their bills before we paid our suppliers. These were lofty goals for such a young company! But little by little, as we proved our ability to maintain our agreements, our suppliers' confidence grew and things became easier."

Bellon discovered that rigorous management is key to the development and longevity of a low-margin business. The necessity of managing every cent on a daily basis quickly became known as the "penny culture" at Sodexho. When a company serves 88,000 meals per day, as was the case for Sodexho at the time, a difference of two cents in the price of a meal makes an enormous difference.

DAILY FOOD COSTS: THE WAR ON EXPENDITURE

"In the accounting department, we had a binder with a section for each site," recalls an employee. "If all our cafeterias could fit into one binder, you know we weren't that big yet.

"So every morning, the site managers would call to report daily spending, the number of meals served, daily food costs and cumulative food costs. The regional manager would regularly come by to check the figures, and he'd call the site managers to tell them, 'You're spending too much'. In general, it was always too much!"

Small Steps, Giant Leaps

As Pierre Bellon often pointed out, a company is a community of people focused on achieving shared objectives. To enable them to do their jobs effectively, the company needs an organization, with structures, compensation policies, human resources and procedures. This is especially challenging for a start-up whose revenues are growing by an average of 40% a year, because the problem is not so much winning new contracts as finding the people to staff them and organize the company.

"I knew all of the site managers and their families when we only had 20 or 30 sites," recalls Bellon, "because I was the one who had hired them. However, I quickly realized I couldn't grow the company by myself. To pursue the development I had in mind, I began hiring people who were smarter than me, or whose strengths complemented mine. The employment market in France was booming in the 1970s and companies were snapping up skilled, valuable people as quickly as they could. When I met with candidates, they often said, 'Sodexho seems like an interesting company to work for. Can you tell me about your career development plan?' To which I would respond, 'We don't have a career development plan. We're growing a young company, which means that I have to trust you and you have to trust me. Ultimately, you will determine your own career development.' And that is exactly what happened. Those brave men and women who joined Sodexho in its early years went on to assume positions of responsibility in Marseilles, Bordeaux, Lyons and Paris. Later on, they would help build Sodexho abroad. Our company was in fact in the business of creating entrepreneurs."

During the early years, mobility was one of the company's underlying principles: employees were expected to be ready to pack their bags on a moment's notice and head off to a new site to spearhead new developments or projects.

While Sodexho benefited from the "fly by the seat of your pants" mentality that is a part of many start-ups, Bellon was also looking beyond a solely action-based approach. He was deeply interested in new organizational design as reflected in his collaboration with Jean Frégnac, beginning in 1962.

At the time, it was rather unusual for a CEO, especially of a small company, to call in a consultant. In fact, Bellon even organized a portside breakfast meeting in Marseilles with his fellow CJD members to explain how to choose a consultant and work effectively with him. He devoured the writings of leading

"An HR director once said, 'Is Sodexho a good company? Yes it is, because it has great people that have helped the company grow.'"

"Pierre Bellon respects and loves people."

Marie-Pierre Le Lohé

American management philosophers, including *The Practice of Management* by Peter Drucker and *The Will to Manage* by Martin Bower, one of the founders of the modern-day consulting industry and chief executive of McKinsey & Co. from the firm's founding in the 1930s until 1963. Both books were later analyzed in executive seminars, which helped to define a certain number of management principles.

Bellon also regularly practiced what would later be known as "benchmarking," "competitive intelligence," and "market research." After visiting Texas Instruments' French operations in Nice in 1968, for example, he and Jean Frégnac came back with the "who, what, when?" method of tracking action plans, which is still used at Sodexho today. "We were always eager to find out what everyone else was doing," recalls Frégnac. "Not many people would have turned to a company like Texas Instruments as a source of inspiration for a company barely two years old, but we were that gutsy!"

In another example, in 1967 Bellon created a market research department, headed by young Planus consultant Marie-Pierre Le Lohé, which soon embarked on a series of studies on remote-site management and food services in France, in Belgium, and in schools and colleges. Over the next two years, the department

THE CREATION OF A MARKET RESEARCH DEPARTMENT

"As a consultant at Planus, I conducted a study on corporate food services in the Paris area for Pierre Bellon," recalls Marie-Pierre Le Lohé. "Outsourcing was a brand-new phenomenon at that time. Bellon called me to say he was happy with my work and wanted to meet for lunch. When we met, he offered me a job at Sodexho. He said, 'Your study was focused on Paris, but I'm interested in going further. I would like to explore opportunities in the Rhône-Alps region, southwestern France and abroad. Since I can't afford the services of a market research company, I've decided to hire someone to do this work on staff. This is the position I'd like you to take on.' In considering his offer, which seemed a bit risky, I told myself that if it didn't work out, I could always leave Sodexho after a couple of years; there were many opportunities available for recent graduates. I joined Sodexho in September 1967 under the impressive title of Head of Market Research. All of our work demonstrated that the market was wide open. It was an exciting experience, but it was also very frustrating, because I realized Sodexho wouldn't be able to follow through on most of the projects we explored. The company simply did not have the resources to hire new people and train them in time to take advantage of all the possibilities the market had to offer. At the end of 1969, Bellon decided to put an end to our work. 'Without the means to exploit these opportunities,' he explained, 'the research does us no good.'" Thus began a new adventure for the young Marie-Pierre, who would take on the responsibility of the public schools food services division.

Raphaël Dubrule

generated so much information that it had to suspend its operations, because Sodexho could not possibly leverage all the opportunities. This ability to experiment with new projects and then step back to evaluate them as needs change or systems prove inadequate would become a lasting hallmark of the company.

Once Sodexho had established its presence throughout France, it began to slowly create its own network of suppliers, a small purchasing department and a financial accounting system.

Upon joining the company in 1969, Albert George took on the massive task of implementing site management tools, including inventories, inventory cards and daily food-cost monitoring for the food services business. Site managers, whose jobs had chiefly consisted of preparing meals and reporting to headquarters, would be held accountable for new procedures. To smooth this transition, Sodexho created a training center for site managers in 1970. The center offered sessions led by Sodexho's corporate executives and outside speakers on administrative work, team management, hygiene, safety and dietary concerns. Sodexho even considered implementing an information technology system, but it was simply too early.

After joining the company as legal and financial advisor in 1969, Raphaël Dubrule tackled the need for a cash-flow management system that would "manage the independence of the different business units while maintaining certain aspects of centralization." Even if the company was decentralized, it still needed appropriate audit and control. Some of the procedures created at this time would be used for 20 years.

"Hello, Marseilles? Philadelphia on the Line."

"Sodexho has enjoyed rapid expansion while maintaining its financial independence over the first five years of its existence, meeting or surpassing all the objectives outlined in its original business plan," states the Board of Directors' 1970 report. The company proved a quick study and the "French campaign" launched by Bellon had enjoyed great success, with nearly 80% revenue growth that year. The company's stellar performance was even making waves on the other side of the Atlantic, as evidenced in a phone call to Bellon at the beginning of 1970.

"Hello? Mr. Bellon?" said a distinctly American voice. "I'll be arriving in Paris in a few days by private jet and would enjoy meeting you. I'm very interested in your company."

Rémi Baudin and Albert George admire the talent of Chef Jean Vanderbeck at Thomson's headquarters in Paris

Pierre Bellon in his office

Bellon was shocked. An American was actually interested in Sodexho?

"May I ask who's calling, Monsieur?"

"My name is Bill Fishman. I'm president and founder of ARA Services[1], the number-one food services company worldwide."

Bill Fishman wasn't kidding around. ARA (Automatic Retailers of America) was the brainchild of Fishman and fellow entrepreneur Dave Davidson. Their company was responsible for the growth of vending machine services in factories and offices in the U.S. and ranked number one in the American market. With a presence on the east and west coasts and in the midwest, ARA Services had recently launched a global initiative. Its first international project was no small feat: the company serviced the 1968 Summer Olympics in Mexico, serving more than a million meals to thousands of competing athletes. Bill was interested in acquiring Sodexho to expand ARA's growth in Europe, where it had entered the English and German markets.

Bellon agreed to meet with Bill Fishman in Paris. Although he wasn't interested in selling his company, he listened attentively to what the American had to say. He even visited ARA in Philadelphia, where he and Rémi Baudin discovered a segmented company

1. ARA Services would become Aramark in 1994.

200 times the size of Sodexho. The two Frenchmen returned home with a wealth of documents, photographs, checklists, procedures and policies. There would be no turning back: it was clear to both men that the food services market held enormous potential. After all, why else would an American leader be interested in their company? Sodexho would not make the mistake of throwing in the towel or ceding to the sweet temptation of diversifying into the commercial food services and hotel businesses, as had Jacques Borel.

Once again, Bellon's foresight was on the mark. Whereas his colleagues had doubted his global vision for the company in 1968, suddenly thinking big and seizing opportunities where American companies had not yet entered the market was the way to go. "If the American food services companies had decided to set up shop in Europe at that time, Sodexho would have been forced out of business," concedes Bellon.

The time had come for Sodexho to launch its international expansion. Other developments soon followed. In 1970, the company moved its general management, corporate departments and head offices for the Paris, West, North and East regions of France to Saint-Cloud, a chic suburb west of Paris. The company was reluctant to move, but the French campaign

"The food services market is an emerging market."

The Executive Committee

Left to right: Raphaël Dubrule, Rémi Baudin, Marie-Françoise de la Fouchardière (Pierre Bellon's assistant), Pierre Bellon, Georges Firmin, Jacques Mesnier, Michel Lorin and André Langlois

needed an extra boost and it would have been very difficult to grow a company headquartered in Marseilles along national, let alone international, lines. The move had its casualties, however. Robert Barthélémy, one of Sodexho's first pioneers and a major contributor to the company's early development in France, refused to leave the port city, and he was not the only one to demonstrate staunch loyalty to the company's birthplace. Even Bellon would continue to use his Marseilles license plates for a long time after leaving the region.

The decision to relocate would prove to be well founded from a strategic point of view. Up to this point, Sodexho had based its development on the acquisition of several leadership positions in local markets, but it had not dominated Paris. It would not be an easy victory. Sodexho would have to fight off powerful competitors such as Borel, who, after securing the number-one position in food services in France with Générale de Restauration, went on to launch the Ticket-Restaurant food voucher program in 1964 and, subsequently, a three-star hotel chain under his name. Sodexho would also have to contend with SHR's 1,000 employees and 50 restaurants, as well as newcomers such as Orly-Restauration, launched in 1969 under the aegis of Maxim's (the famous three-star

Paris restaurant), and Eurest, created in 1970 by two powerful, prestigious players, Compagnie des Wagons-Lits and Nestlé, the latter offering a major advantage due to its significant European presence.

The food services era had begun.

"Sodexho is no more, no less
than the community
of its clients and customers,
employees and shareholders"

*

Making organic growth
a top priority

From 1966 to 1970, Sodexho's revenues grew by a factor of six, from 1.04 to 6.47 million euros, at an average annual growth rate of 58%. Net income increased by a factor of five, from 25,000 to 120,000 euros, at an average annual growth rate of 48%.

Second Era (1970–1983)

THE PATH OF PROGRESS

"As soon as Sodexho expanded nationally, I started to think about international prospects."

Sodexho spent much of the 1970s pursuing its recently launched meal voucher activities[1] and new client segments – education, healthcare and onshore and offshore remote sites – in the food services business. "As I remained committed to developing Sodexho," explains Pierre Bellon, "I started looking for two types of growth opportunity: new geographical markets and new client segments. To this day, market segmentation continues to allow us to grow."

From Europe to Latin America and from French Polynesia to the Middle East, Sodexho expanded its reach, adapting its offering to the needs of its clients wherever they were and dealing with the inevitable challenges as the company continued to expand. By the early 1980s, Sodexho was active in every major sector it serves today. Eight years after launching its first international operations, Sodexho was operating in 35 countries, earning 55% of its revenues abroad, with more than 15,000 employees, of which 8,000 were based outside of France. After enduring a thrilling battle for control of its historic rival, Jacques Borel International, Sodexho was listed on the Paris Stock Exchange in 1983.

1. Intended for companies without any on-site food services, meal vouchers are a form of employer-subsidized compensation that enable employees to pay for meals in local restaurants.

4

_____Sodexho the Conqueror_____

Pierre Bellon's visit to the U.S. marked a milestone in Sodexho's history, as it exponentially increased his ambitions for the company.

Sodexho would naturally pursue growth in France, where the market was full of opportunities. But because it sought to expand in a sector where growth is directly linked to the number of inhabitants – with France only representing 1% of the world's population – it would also start looking beyond the country's borders, launching an international initiative in the early 1970s that would take it from Belgium's wintry frosts to the wild jungles of Africa in less than ten years.

Gaining Ground in Hospitals and Schools

"I came back from the U.S. convinced that we had to focus on the vast opportunities in the food services market," recalls Bellon. His visit to the American

"Our future was determined the moment I realized that France, despite being the fourth-largest economy, represented less than 1% of the world's population."

"When we begin working with a new company, school or hospital, we need to have people within the organization with whom we can exchange ideas; our goal is not to replace our clients but to provide specialized services to help them get things done."

market leader Aramark confirmed the intuition on which Sodexho had been founded, proving wrong the one or two naysayers who did not believe in the market's growth prospects.

It was true that competition had become increasingly entrenched and specialized companies had blossomed in a sector that had not existed just a few years earlier, but the market was far from saturated. Only a mere 5% – or 500,000 – of the 10 million meals served outside the home in France were provided by food services companies. Outsourcing was a far from common practice, and even the press was using terms such as canteens and eateries. The concept of the customer as guest was yet to come.

In the early 1970s, only 16% of companies relied on third-party service providers to serve meals on-site to their employees. Nevertheless, outsourcing was clearly the wave of the future. French companies were increasingly eliminating the traditional practice of closing for lunch, while new business districts, like La Défense west of Paris, and office towers, like the Tour Montparnasse, were sprouting at a dizzying pace. In addition, the first new towns were being built in the outer suburbs of the country's largest cities, attracting

THE "LUSITANIA" PLAN

No blow was too low among companies looking to increase their share of the food services market. Sodexho's biggest competitors were no exception; they would aim to hit where it hurt most, going after Sodexho's employees, the mainstay of the company.

One morning, Pierre Bellon received an anonymous package, dated February 2, 1972. The envelope contained a detailed analysis of Sodexho's activities and operations as well as an action plan aimed at destabilizing the company.

The "Lusitania" plan, as it was called, had been designed at the behest of Jacques Borel by a former Sodexho employee who was hired by the competition after being laid off by Sodexho. Sent by someone outraged at Borel's approach, the document outlined a plan to poach certain regional directors, site managers and directors who had been identified as pillars of the company.

But Borel would have as little success convincing Sodexho employees to join his company – not a single manager would choose to leave – as he would in maintaining control of his own firm, which would later be bought out.

It is interesting to note that, among the ten leading food services providers at the time, only Sodexho would maintain the same ownership through the years, whereas the other nine would be bought out one or more times.

a growing number of companies to their greenfield sites. Demand for outsourced food services could only increase.

The battle for Paris proved just as difficult as Bellon had foreseen, and Sodexho, a newcomer to the region's competitive landscape, had a rough time signing on corporate clients. While the company had been busy building a stronghold in the provinces, its competitors had solidified their positions in the vast Paris market. Market leader Jacques Borel and European outsider Eurest were already aggressively canvassing the market of corporate headquarters and office blocks where the concept of a multi-tenant cafeteria serving several companies was booming.

Corporate clients, however appealing, represented only one segment of the food services market. The education and healthcare sectors, where outsourcing was still extremely rare, also offered vast opportunities to those willing to try their luck.

As Sodexho began looking at these market segments, it would discover that healthcare and educational clients had very different needs when compared to the company's clients in business and industry. Sodexho's early experience working with schools and hospitals, which brought it into daily contact with hospital managers and boarding school stewards, would prove to be an invaluable training ground. During this period, the company would build its expertise and develop a range that quickly grew from food services to a more diverse offering.

When Sodexho first contracted with schools, only 0.5% of educational institutions were outsourcing food services to third-party providers. The market was ripe with opportunity, but the battle was still far from won. Sodexho may have specialized in food services, but the company was still quite young. It would have its job cut out for itself in trying to convince decision-makers, many of whom were content with the status quo, to hand over responsibility for serving meals to children.

Sodexho launched 11 new school cafeterias in 1971, working closely with nutritionists to create menus and keeping an open dialogue with teachers, supervisors and the city halls that ran the schools. The company built its expertise by staying close to its clients and the children it was feeding, whose needs differed from those of Sodexho's other clients. "My first client was a junior high school located in a Paris suburb," recalls Marie-Pierre Le Lohé, who took on the responsibility of developing educational food services in the Ile-de-France (Greater Paris) region in 1971. "I had to report to the head of the city's main kitchen[1], which served about 4,000 meals a day. Impressed by how well he knew his job, I wanted to work closely with him, so I started to visit him regularly, almost once a week, spending an afternoon with him each

A school cafeteria in the town of Salon-de-Provence, France, 1973

1. Food supplies were stocked in these central facilities, where meals were prepared and packaged before being delivered to the sites where they were served.

BEHIND THE SCENES AT THE HÔTEL DIEU HOSPITAL

One Thursday in 1973, Albert George, head of Sodexho's operations in Paris, received an urgent phone call from the superintendent of the Hôtel Dieu hospital. The kitchen ceiling of the magnificent edifice – whose oldest sections date back to King Louis IX – had just caved in. "The person in charge of Paris' public hospital system is going to ask you to provide a temporary meal delivery service starting Monday," said the superintendent. Not including breakfast, the service amounted to 1,800 meals per day. Food was prepared in Sodexho's main facilities in Saint-Cloud and delivered hot to the hospital kitchen, amidst the rubble, where it was arranged on patient trays or served to employees, in a space exposed to the elements and birds. Originally intended as an emergency service that would last 45 days while the kitchen was being repaired, Sodexho wound up delivering meals to the hospital for three to four years!

Albert George

time. He taught me all he knew about food services in public schools, including the importance of the cafeteria environment and nutrition."

In the 1970s, Sodexho also secured its first food services contracts with hospitals, a rare feat in a market reluctant to outsource its operations to third-party service providers.

Thanks to these first experiences with healthcare clients, Sodexho continued to build its food services expertise. Its contract with Marseilles' La Timone hospital, beginning at the end of 1973 and serving

6,000 meals a day, proved to be a real-life experience from which the company was able to draw many lessons. The same year, Sodexho began operating food services at the Brabois hospital in Nancy, in northeastern France.

Despite a difficult economic situation in France at the time, Sodexho was able to enjoy its first successes in the healthcare sector, which only proved that the market was full of opportunities. Nonetheless, price controls and inflation cut profits for Sodexho and other players in the market. The financial magazine *L'Expansion* ran an article titled, "You Don't Make Much Dough in a Cafeteria," which read, "That's how things go: you can pile high mountains of grated carrots but you'll never heap up profits bigger than a molehill." And that molehill would shrink even further during periods of heavy inflation, when net margins of 1–2% would fall below the 1% mark.

Gradually, a buying system took shape for dealing with escalating ingredient prices, which represented approximately 50% of production costs. Created in 1974, the SOCAP (Central Procurement Company) brought together specialized buyers who were responsible for negotiating prices and listing products and qualified suppliers. The heads of various sites would order supplies from these SOCAP suppliers

A hospital dining hall, France

The Grand Place in Brussels, Belgium, where Sodexho would begin its European expansion

and buying was managed at the regional level. "This system allowed us to work with industrial-sized wholesalers," explains Bellon. "This helped us to streamline our infrastructure and increase our financial freedom by avoiding the high costs of carrying inventory."

Despite a multitude of opportunities on the French market, however, it would not be vast enough to secure Sodexho's future, and the company started looking toward neighboring countries.

Early Days in Europe

Convinced that there was a significant common ground between Belgium and France, Sodexho chose to launch its European initiative just across the border. The company would soon discover, however, that Belgium was anything but a small version of France. Renowned for its french fries, Belgian cuisine had culinary traditions in its own right, including such specialties as *waterzooï* (creamy stews) and *briquet* sandwiches (lighter fare). The country was further characterized by its two distinct languages and cultures.

Sodexho's partnership with Société Générale de Belgique, the country's leading private sector company, resulted in the creation of a Belgian subsidiary in 1970.

Unfortunately, the French management team that was sent to develop business in Belgium had little success. Even the team's main members admit that Sodexho's early days in the market were a disaster, as the company racked up one error after another. The menus were created in France and the food itself was French. Using the latest regithermic techniques, Sodexho employees would prepare meals in a central facility belonging to the client and then transport them to the client site once the meals had been chilled; they were then reheated just prior to being served. This procedure proved to be ill-suited for the situation. The french fries became soggy and the over-cooked meat of Bellon's early days in the food services industry reared its ugly head once again! A few weeks later, after meeting with an unhappy client, Bellon decided to place Rémi Baudin, managing director of Sodexho's French operations at the time, at the head of the Belgian subsidiary.

A few months later, Sodexho signed a food services contract with NATO in Brussels, marking its true beginning in Belgium. More importantly, however, the company had learned, albeit the hard way, a very vital lesson that it would not forget: there are as many different approaches to food services as there are local cultures.

"You are what you eat."

From Italy to Brazil via Australia, Sodexho adopted an approach that would drive its success and elevate it to being a truly global company, long before the concept of globalization had become widely understood. This approach hinged on hiring and training local employees in every market where Sodexho sought to expand its operations.

After Belgium, Sodexho eyed the Italian market, where two of its major competitors, Jacques Borel and Eurest, had established themselves and were serving 50,000 meals a day. It seemed unlikely that Sodexho would be able to catch up if it were to start from square one. So Bellon followed the advice of the head of Société Générale Italy, and contacted the editor-in-chief of a local restaurant magazine to inquire about small, successful companies ready to be acquired.

Sodexho thus took over Italmense, a highly reputable family business, and launched operations in Italy at the level of 10,000 meals a day. Eager to avoid making the same mistakes it had made in Belgium, Sodexho quickly hired Italian managers, including Giacomo Sorlini, who eventually became president of Sodexho in Italy. These early recruits were responsible for catapulting the subsidiary into the leadership position in the Italian market.

ITALY'S FIRST IN-HOUSE FOOD SERVICES TRAINING PROGRAM

In the late 1970s, Italmense was the first and only food services company with an in-house training program. In a market where hotel management programs were few and far between, Sodexho faced a lack of specialized training and serious difficulties in hiring skilled people. The subsidiary adopted an innovative practice of offering theoretical and practical internships to recent college graduates. Hailed by local authorities and the food services sector as a whole, these training courses would lead to the creation of an in-house training center a few months later. The center's reputation for excellence earned it financial support from the European community and it was praised to such an extent that Italmense's competitors asked that their employees be permitted to participate.

The Banco di Roma's dining hall, Italy

Giacomo Sorlini

The oil-drilling platform *Neptune*
in the Gulf of Guinea

Crossing Paths with Elephants and New Cultures

The early 1970s also marked the launch of Sodexho's operations in Africa.

After securing a contract in Gabon, Sodexho's French client ETPM asked Sodexho to operate one of its oil barges in the region. Sodexho was eager to comply, for opportunities in Africa were rapidly multiplying thanks to businesses growing around the continent's oil resources.

Sodexho very quickly expanded into other countries, notably Cameroon and the Republic of Congo. One factor that stood out was the mobility of the barges that Sodexho served – they could drill for one or two months in Gabon before moving on to the Democratic Republic of Congo.

In Africa as elsewhere, Sodexho grew its business by following its clients to fresh markets. The company's first experiences on a new continent, with its different, often harsh working conditions, were characterized by the same trial-and-error experience typical of ventures into new territory. But thanks to vast opportunities for further business, Sodexho was quickly able to welcome fresh clients into its fold – and enjoy the profits they brought with them.

Other operations were quickly developed, from food and other corporate services to the management of remote sites, where working conditions were as tough and colorful as on the oil barges Sodexho supported. The Gamba camp, located in the middle of the jungle at the edge of a lagoon, halfway between Port-Gentil and Pointe-Noire in Gabon, was not accessible by motor vehicle. There were only two ways to get there: via a small plane, with a flying time of one hour and 15 minutes, or via a flat-bottomed boat, with a sailing time of 30 hours across ocean and lagoon. At this out-of-the-ordinary site, where elephants would sometimes block the landing strip, Sodexho managed a hotel-camp, a dining facility and diverse services such as cleaning, security, laundry, entertainment and maintenance. The company was also responsible for overseeing the distribution and sales of food and other essential items.

Using the local hiring practices it had tested in Europe proved to be a major challenge for Sodexho in Africa, but the company stuck to its guns, training and trusting people in local markets, a philosophy that would become a major driver of its growth. Long before today's vision of "sustainable development" had been conceived, Sodexho was providing opportunities for local employees to advance in the company's

The Gamba camp is supplied by flat-bottomed boat, Gabon

On a landing strip in Africa

MANAGING IN AFRICA

"Throughout Africa, Sodexho operations managers had to be completely independent," recalls Michel Fruchard, who found the African experience to be highly rewarding. "Client interactions took on a completely different dimension than they had in France, and all of us expats shared a close bond due to our being isolated and carrying similar burdens of having to manage on our own. Working together as client and supplier, we joined forces to overcome the challenges of the African market. Operations managers had to be skilled at delegating, work autonomously, and derive genuine satisfaction from being able to resolve a tricky problem or difficult situation on their own. Of course, team efforts played a major role, but the responsibilities of each individual were much greater in Africa."

Pierre Bellon, N. Kewbé,
Michel Landel, Bruno Chauliac,
Patrice Douce and Philippe Voraz

organizational structure. "Highly reputed, Sodexho benefits from the positive image enjoyed by food services providers in Africa," said Yves Bayon, head of operations in Gabon, in 1977. "Following a training period, a number of the company's African employees have been given increasing responsibility and have advanced up the rungs of the corporate ladder."

Africa offered exciting career opportunities to young managers willing to take on new responsibilities, including Philippe Voraz, who would later become president, South America and Turkey Food

1992: SODEXHO NIGERIA CELEBRATES ITS TENTH ANNIVERSARY

People who attended Sodexho Nigeria's tenth anniversary party still have vivid memories of that colorful event. Employees, clients, prospects and suppliers were invited to the celebration, which was also an occasion to honor Puis Okou, the local cook with the most seniority, and Chineye Ihenebo, who was hired to wash dishes and worked his way up to become camp manager. But the awards didn't stop there. Pierre Bellon was officially made a "Chief" by Chief A. A. A. Shasanya,

Sodexho's partner in Nigeria at the time. To abide by traditional practices, Bellon was asked to exchange his suit and tie for a kind of Scottish kilt and bowler hat and hold a long cane, symbol of his new rank.

Pierre Bellon wearing
the traditional costume
of a Nigerian tribal chief

and Management Services, Nicolas Japy, who would become group COO and CEO, Remote Sites and Asia-Australia Food and Management Services, and Michel Landel, who ultimately rose to the position of Sodexho CEO.

Sodexho's headquarters in Saint Cloud, just west of Paris, 1972

"We Almost Went Under"

At the end of 1973, the atmosphere at Sodexho's headquarters in Saint-Cloud was filled with anxiety, as the company faced a possible cash shortage stemming from contracts with several state-owned companies. "At the beginning of the year," explains Pierre Bellon, "I told the top three French banks I was looking to develop our activities in the public sector. To do so, we would need to borrow approximately 1.5 million euros in working capital. All of the bankers told me the same thing: 'You are always worried about not having enough money, Monsieur Bellon. If you need to borrow money, we will lend it to you.' When I went back to them in October, I was stunned to learn that, due to credit control measures implemented by the Finance Minister, they were unable to offer any credit facilities."

"As long as our cash flow was positive," recalls Bernard Carton, then chief financial officer, "bankers would come to woo Bellon and ask him to borrow money. And then the day he really needed money, while waiting for certain public hospitals to pay their bills, they cut us off." It would take a month of negotiations for Bellon to finally obtain the credit facilities he needed.

The credit crunch forced Sodexho into a state of emergency, as it put in place strict contractual definitions for means of payment, stringent instructions for sales teams, decisive actions for cash collection from healthcare clients and extensions of supplier credit. Within six months, things had calmed down and Sodexho's position had stabilized. "We almost went under," admits Bellon. But Sodexho's managers learned a valuable lesson from the crisis, and careful financial mastery of growth would become one of the company's underlying principles. "It was a good experience," concedes Bellon, "because it taught me not to depend on banks for short-term solutions. We adopted a simple strategy of choosing activities with low capital intensity, maintaining a certain level of cash in hand by engaging in operations that do not require working capital and by borrowing mid- to long-term. We follow the same strategy today."

The experience also led Sodexho to adopt another underlying principle of the company: that of balancing risk. The company would address the notion of geographical risk by stepping up its expansion outside France, but it would also look to diversify its client base and markets by seeking new growth drivers.

Bernard Carton

At the same time, Bellon decided that, to obtain the financial resources needed for growth, the company should go public. He asked chief financial officer Bernard Carton and executive vice president Raphaël Dubrule to begin preparing the company for listing on the Paris Stock Exchange. "We were delighted to be working with him on the listing," recalls Dubrule, "but as you can imagine, we were also laughing to ourselves because Sodexho was such a small company!"

After surviving its first serious crisis, Sodexho ended up stronger and more determined than ever to overcome the challenges and risks standing in the way of its growth. It began to look to the desert sands and the oil wells that were starting to shake up most of the world's economies, kicking off a mad rush for oil. From Saudi Arabia to the North Sea by way of Gabon, new companies were springing up everywhere, specializing in geological research, drilling, construction of marine infrastructure, oil production and refining. And with the growth of these companies and their ranks would come a demand for reception facilities and food services.

5

_____ The Black Gold Rush _____

From Africa to the Middle East and to the North Sea, "oil" was the magic word that fueled Sodexho's first phase of growth in remote-site management services. Upon launching its first operations in Africa in the early 1970s and in the Middle East in 1974, Sodexho would position itself and build relationships that would enable it to become the global leader in that field within a decade. It would also have what it needed to survive the second oil crisis, which led to the downfall of many less stable competitors.

Remote-site management services on land and sea would prove to be a valuable growth engine in Sodexho's expansion, as Pierre Bellon had foreseen early on. Representing as much as 55% of Sodexho's operating income, it would allow the company to finance its growth strategy through the beginning of the 1980s.

"In remote sites in the middle of the desert or surrounded by forest, on oil platforms in the middle of the sea, beneath often sweltering skies…"

In Chile, the illustrator for
the employee newspaper tells
the tale of Sodexho's rise
to prominence

1976. Abela leads the pack in a luxurious horse-drawn coach, followed by SHRM's buggy and Grand Met, the forerunner of Compass, in a black Jaguar. Far in the distance, Sodexho tries desperately to catch up to the three leaders. The other market players are so insignificant that they do not appear.

1981. A modern, upscale Abela is tailed by the Italian Liguabue on a motorcycle, followed by Grand Met. SHRM is starting to lose pace with its competitors, as is Eurest, on a scooter. Despite considerable progress, Sodexho remains at the tail end of the pack.

1986. Now the leader, Sodexho tows Portuguese competitor Catermar, followed by a broken-down SHRM. Abela is losing speed and Grand Met is running out of breath, with Eurest and Liguabue far behind.

An oil well in the Sahara Desert

The Sands of the Sahara

But remote sites had made their appearance much earlier in the life of Pierre Bellon, who had first experienced them in the Sahara Desert.

In 1958, the decolonization movement was already well on its way in Algeria when Félix Bellon, in association with two partners, created SGR, a company specializing in supplying French oil companies in the Sahara Desert. It was a time of rapid development in the oil and gas industries despite political uncertainties; within ten years, global production had doubled. It was a veritable oil boom.

With an uncertain future for the family's shipping business, Pierre Bellon's father saw the Sahara Desert's growing oil trade as an opportunity to diversify and strengthen his company. Entering the market would be even more challenging, given that Sodexho's Marseilles rival SHRM had established a solid market position ten years earlier.

Only a few months after joining the family company, 28-year-old Pierre Bellon found himself jointly managing SGR with two partners, ages 70 and 65. Their attempt at three-way management proved quite difficult, given their highly divergent political views: one partner believed Algeria should remain a French colony; the other held much more extreme views, supporting the secret OAS army fighting to maintain French rule in Algeria; while Bellon was convinced that Algerian independence was inevitable. Needless to say, the decision-making process was anything but smooth, and Bellon resolved "never again to get involved in a company where management is split between three different families – it is a sure recipe for disaster."

But SGR continued to pursue operations until Algerian independence was declared, and even after 1962 despite difficult conditions. With the creation of Algeria's national oil company Sonatrach in 1963, however, Bellon was convinced that SGR could not survive, as the public company would slowly take business away from the French oil companies. In order to have free rein to decide the company's future, he encouraged his father, along with a friend, to buy out the other two families, whose representatives had already returned to France.

Bellon also convinced his family to join forces with Sonatrach; he believed it to be the only way of saving SGR and its 350 employees from a fate similar to that of SHRM, which had shut down abruptly without any concern for its workers. Hired in 1965 to run the supply business and oversee SGR's operations in Algeria, Rémi Baudin thus began a long negotiation

A remote site in the Sahara Desert

process in late 1967 that ended on June 27, 1969 with the signing of an agreement between Bellon and Sonatrach president Ahmed Ghozali. Sonatrach became a 60% shareholder in SGR, and the new company, named Alrah, would be run by an Algerian president, with Rémi Baudin serving as CEO.

Sodexho signed a technical support contract with Alrah to assist in the transition to Algerian management and the company's growth in the region's remote-site market. At the end of its contract two years later, Sodexho pulled out of the company and the Bellon family sold its 40% holding to Sonatrach. It took a long time for the paperwork to go through, but the funds were finally transferred to France at the end of 1976. Alrah would become one of the rare foreign companies created before 1962 to be bought out and paid for by the Algerian government, thanks to the quality of relations between outgoing and incoming teams.

With SGR and then Alrah, Bellon was able to observe the advent of major oil companies en masse and the economic development they generated. He was convinced that things were going to happen in the Middle East and he was right: the region, with its multicultural heritage, would prove to be the

ALRAH OR ALEXHO?

"One Friday, the head of SGR called to tell us that the Sonatrach president's right-hand man wanted to meet us in Algiers the following Monday at 11 o'clock," recalls Rémi Baudin. "Pierre Bellon was already committed to attending a conference at the CJD all weekend long and would not be able to leave before Monday morning. The first flight on Monday was scheduled to arrive in Algiers at 11:30 and the meeting could not be pushed back, so we rented a small plane, which represented a huge expense for Sodexho!

"Upon our arrival, we were informed that the point of the meeting was to decide on a name for our future joint company. 'You have suggested Alexho, but we prefer Alrah.' Stunned, we gave in to the Sonatrach representative's wishes, and after five minutes the meeting was over. We had received no information whatsoever regarding the timetable of events and were left with nothing to do but wait for the evening flight, which was much cheaper than flying by private plane!"

remote-site market in which Sodexho would develop its operations.

Shifting Sands

Despite warnings from his bankers, who strongly discouraged him from pursuing development in the Middle East, Bellon asked Indosuez, a French bank well established in the Middle East, to find a partner

A barbecue held in the desert for employees of the Saudi Arabian subsidiary in 1981. Pierre Bellon and Patrice Douce are talking to Abdallah al-Shahrani, head of sales in Saudi Arabia, in the presence of several other employees.

for Sodexho in Saudi Arabia. He also named Patrice Douce – who had just spent two years in Gabon – to head the project.

A few months after sending the young man to Jeddah at the end of 1973, Bellon founded Sodexho's Saudi Arabian subsidiary through an agreement with Mr. Abbar and Mr. Zainy, two highly reputed Saudi Arabian businessmen whom he had met through Indosuez. Each partner would hold 50% of the company's capital of 92,000 euros. Sodexho's partnership with a national player would prove to be a decisive factor in the company's development in Saudi Arabia.

"Just before signing," recalls Bellon, "Ahmed Zainy, the head of the family, said, 'I'm ready to sign but I want some kind of guarantee. I am risking 46,000 euros in a venture that you will be managing. I don't want to lose my money.' I understood where he was coming from, so I offered him Sodexho's guarantee. He refused, saying, 'What I want is your personal guarantee.' It was at that moment that I realized our relationship was based on mutual trust, so I agreed. I didn't regret it, because within six months, the venture had already earned the equivalent of our initial investment."

Sodexho's business in Saudi Arabia took off, despite serious competition from the Lebanese company Abela (which had a network of subsidiaries throughout the Middle East), SHRM and Grand Met, forerunner of the U.K.-based Compass food services group, one of Sodexho's major competitors today. After signing its first contract in Jeddah with Bouygues, a French construction and public works company, Sodexho opened three offices – first in Jeddah, then in Riyadh and Dhahran – to handle business throughout the country. "We grew very rapidly," recalls Douce, laughing. "We were making a lot of money, earning 200% of the group's profits in the Middle East alone!"

Patrice Douce

Despite the attractive financial packages offered to Sodexho employees abroad, qualified candidates were hard to find and skilled labor was lacking on-site. "We were in need of site managers and operations managers, but the hot weather and distance made recruitment difficult. We managed to get around the shortage of labor, but not without some very trying moments," says Douce.

To respond to the specific needs of the sector and to support operations in the Middle East, a back-office support service was set up in Montigny, France in 1977, headed by Anne-Marie Maisonnave, who had been with Sodexho since 1970 and now had an

Anne-Marie Maisonnave
with young Peul women in Mali

opportunity to experience firsthand the organizational beginnings of the Oil and Large Projects division, the ancestor of today's remote-site management business. "We had to hire a lot of people, manage teams and coordinate sales efforts," she remembers. "We also had to find kitchen equipment and food suppliers." Soon thereafter, Maisonnave would head to Iraq, where she would oversee Sodexho's operations and confront the challenges of working in the Middle East.

One of the first players in the region's remote-site market, Sodexho based its expansion on a principle of trust in its young managers, who were equally motivated by the unique experience of working in the Middle East and by the prospect of learning and growing with the company. Thanks to the solid relationships it built with local contacts, Sodexho managed to survive, even in the midst of difficult economic circumstances.

Competition increased from 1978 on, with more than 100 service providers of all nationalities and sizes up and running on the Saudi Arabian market alone. And along with the growth of the sector came merciless price wars. To prepare for increasingly difficult

A WOMAN IN IRAQ

Anne-Marie Maisonnave transferred to Iraq in November 1979 and remained there until April 1982. War broke out in September 1980. "It was a strange time," she recalls. "When we signed a contract with a public works company in Iraq to build the Baghdad airport, Patrice Douce asked me if I wanted to participate in that project. Immediately thereafter, we began working with Bouygues, which was building a factory in Iraq. As supervisor, my first task was to seek potential suppliers. A French-speaking Iraqi buyer for Bouygues helped me out by introducing me to his suppliers. Surprisingly enough, I didn't encounter a single problem as a woman dealing with Iraqis. They may have been taken aback, but they were always kind."

market conditions, Sodexho lowered prices, sometimes by as much as 40%, and reduced costs by accelerating the training and promotion of local employees.

The Iranian revolution, the Iran–Iraq war and OPEC's decision to decrease oil production resulted in a second oil crisis. In Saudi Arabia, which had decreased daily oil production from 10 million to 4.5 million barrels, a number of major projects were cancelled or delayed. Sodexho nonetheless managed to pull through the crisis without much difficulty. "The sector is of course suffering from economic recession and increased levels of competition, but the price decreases demanded by clients have caused many less competitive food services companies to go out of business. Fortunately enough, these failures have allowed Sodexho to grow," states the Board of Directors' report to the Shareholders Meeting for fiscal year 1982.

On the Deep, Dark Sea

Far from the desert sands, Sodexho would also play a role in the hunt for oil and gas in the North Sea. In 1975 it created a subsidiary in Aberdeen, Scotland, the region's main center for oil drilling.

Offshore exploration, begun after World War II in the shallow waters of the Gulf of Mexico, would be driven by constantly increasing demand from the Persian Gulf and the shores of Africa to the deeper, more hostile waters of the North and Labrador Seas.

Sodexho's level of activity in the North Sea fluctuated a great deal throughout the 1980s, in tandem with the difficulties facing the local offshore drilling industry and the evolving price of crude oil. Heavy investments in infrastructure and facilities were necessitated by the fact that oil fields were often divided between several bordering countries. This was the case for the U.K., with back-office support services in Aberdeen, Scotland, and Norway, with a base in

LIFE ABOARD THE *1601* BARGE

The ETPM 1601 crane and pipe-laying vessel was 55,000 tons of steel anchored in the middle of the North Sea, off the coast of Norway. The floating factory housed 340 people – including 30 Sodexho employees overseeing a full range of services – living underwater and by artificial light. Working in two shifts of 12 hours each, employees on the barge had trouble distinguishing night from day.

On board, everything was constantly in motion. At any given moment, there could be a pressure cooker and a fried steak on the stove in the kitchen; in the gangway, a cabin boy, his arms full of sheets; at the bar, people playing foosball; and on the deck, a welder at work asking what the day's menu was. In the four-man cabins, however, the only sounds were the fragmented conversations of those who had just finished a shift and were getting ready for bed, those who were getting up to start their workday, and those who, asleep for the past hour, had just been awakened by their cabin mates!

The ETPM 1601 barge

Stavanger. But competition was strong, especially from the U.S. and the U.K., with no less than 20 food services companies working on the North Sea's oil platforms in the early 1980s. Price wars led to a rapid decrease in earnings and serious losses, at which point Sodexho placed its North Sea operations on hold. But the company did not give up on the market entirely and returned to the region in the mid-1990s.

For pioneers like Sodexho, the 1980 oil crisis marked the end of an era. As Sodexho's senior executives had predicted, a golden age had come and gone and it was time to turn to new opportunities.

6

Sodexho's
——— Expanding Presence ———

Once it had regained its financial stability, Sodexho consolidated its existing operations, pursued its growth strategy, and explored new markets to avoid being overly dependent on any one client segment.

Meanwhile, in France...

Once the crisis of 1973 had passed, Sodexho began to focus on its future growth.

A marketing manager position was created in 1976 to keep up with rapid growth in the education segment. That same year, Sodexho hired a dietitian, whose main responsibilities included running meetings in which menus were determined, and site managers were

"Each customer and site was unique."

educated on the importance of a balanced diet and on adapting menus to the needs of children. "Sodexho was far ahead of its time, because it was concerned about food quality early on and did not hesitate to hire nutrition and health specialists," recalls a company dietitian. "We created activities and workshops tailored to the education sector. Luckily for us, our site managers and clients were receptive to the ideas we presented, as they already recognized the importance of nutrition. It was harder to address companies, however, since our approach was entirely new to them. Nevertheless, we managed to implement such campaigns as 'A Vegetarian Theme' and 'Keeping Fit.'" Sodexho was also one of the first companies in the sector to implement bacteriological testing on all of the ingredients it used and the food it served.

Sodexho also began looking at opportunities in the seniors segment and, by the end of 1982, it was running 33 cafeterias in homes for the elderly. The company's offering ranged from preparing and serving meals to organizing and overseeing a full array of services tailored to the needs of seniors living in retirement homes.

As unassuming as it seems, Sodexho was learning how to do its job as it evolved, often working closely with its clients to hone skills sets that would eventually help it to dominate the market. Given that each customer and site was highly unique, the company would come to benefit from a diverse body of expertise. Sodexho's offering would grow to include a mosaic of services that went as far as needed to meet its clients' expectations. Not only was Pierre Bellon innovative enough to have this vision, but he also knew how to show his employees ways in which to adopt it as their own. "Food service is at the heart of how people work and live together because it affects employees at work, children at school and patients in hospital. It represents an increasingly important factor in the daily lives of more than one-quarter of the French population. Our continued attempts to improve service quality allow us to contribute to improvements in quality of life," declared Bellon in 1976. Thanks to the astuteness of its founder, Sodexho was benefiting from wisdom far beyond its years. After all, how many companies were looking to improve quality of life 30 years ago?

Thanks in part to the work of Jean-Michel Dhenain, Sodexho launched a sales division at the end of 1974, first as a pilot in southeastern France and then throughout the country, to reinforce sales efforts and create a more specialized sales force. "Throughout the mid-1970s," explains Jacques Tavel, "the various

Jean-Michel
Dhenain

Company headquarters in Montigny-le-Bretonneux, southwest of Paris, 1977

regional branches were responsible for all aspects of the business, including bringing in new clients, managing operations and hiring new employees. One day, we realized that we couldn't be good at everything. We had to choose between being excellent operators and so-so business developers." Due to the high level of autonomy within the corporate culture, Sodexho regional directors were responsible for units that increasingly resembled small, separate companies.

While the role of managers as independent entrepreneurs in a decentralized organization had long been part of Sodexho's corporate DNA, now they were also being encouraged to become more professional. By 1976, Sodexho – which could be described as a "large federation of artisans" – had more than 9,000 employees. To keep up with the growth, the company headquarters was moved from Saint Cloud to Montigny-le-Bretonneux, a business district in the new town of Saint-Quentin-en-Yvelines, southwest of Paris, close to Versailles.

Sodexho's attempts to grow its operations in new client segments were certainly paying off, as the company saw average business-volume increases of 30% annually throughout the 1970s. In 1981, Sodexho topped the ranks of France's food services providers, beating out Générale de Restauration for the first time.

According to the Pioneers

The late 1970s also marked Sodexho's return to Brazil, which had remained dear to Bellon's heart despite a ten-year absence.

Created in 1977 by a team of expatriates that would gradually be phased out and replaced with local employees, Sodexho's Brazilian subsidiary signed its first contract in 1979. Three years later, it would already be managing 16 cafeterias in state-owned and private companies, including several banks. The Brazilian market was brimming with opportunity, but, like most of South America in the late 1970s and early 1980s, it was also subject to chronic hyperinflation, which sometimes reached levels of 30-40% per month! Faced with a series of losses despite satisfactory business development, Bellon scheduled a meeting with his Brazilian management team in Sao Paulo in May 1982 that would go down in the company's history. His message was clear: "Gentlemen, you have seen me samba. You know how much I love Brazil. It's a young country with brilliant prospects. We will never leave Brazil as we might leave other foreign countries, but now it's up to you. I am not going to invest a single cent more in this business." Bellon kept

THE MYTH OF THE CENTRAL KITCHEN

Known as the Promised Land of South America thanks to its oil resources, Venezuela was working on a number of immense projects in several sectors, including food services. At least, that is what Sodexho believed when it got wind of a project undertaken by the Department of Education and the Health Department to build a central kitchen that would prepare all the food served in the Caracas public school system. At the very least, the contract would be worth 200,000 meals a day! Sodexho immediately mobilized teams dedicated to the project, including a design department, directors and project managers. A large contingent of the country's civil servants came all the way to France to verify Sodexho's expertise. But alas, as Sodexho would later discover, the Venezuelans were actually spies sent by international competitors in Venezuela to gather confidential information about the company. Sodexho would spend about 152,000 euros on this project, which never did see the light of day.

his promise and his surprising approach worked: Sodexho's Brazilian subsidiary realized its first profits the following year.

At the same time, Sodexho was reviewing opportunities in other South American countries. After scouting out the Venezuelan and Argentine markets, however, it decided to delay its expansion in South America, which was suffering from an unprecedented economic crisis. Sodexho would instead focus its energies on Brazil, and then Chile, where it created a subsidiary in 1981.

In entering the Chilean market, where American player Marriott was already managing 100 cafeterias in the capital city of Santiago, Bellon tried to adopt the same strategy that had proven successful in other countries with competition. He began to search for a small local food-services company to acquire, but after weeks of negotiations, an earthquake and difficulties between the company's prospective partner and Chilean authorities, Sodexho shifted its strategy and launched a food services business on its own.

When Bellon handed Yves Bayon the keys to Sodexho's Chilean subsidiary, he said, ' I'm giving you a million francs (152,000 euros). Now it's up to you."

"We began from nothing," recalls Dominique Brillaud, who was appointed head of the subsidiary by Bayon, later becoming head of purchasing for Sodexho's French operations. "And when I say 'nothing,' that is exactly what I mean. We had to do everything ourselves, from canvassing potential clients to making ourselves known and growing the business. We managed our projects, went to see prospective clients and even cleaned the office ourselves. It wasn't always easy

Yves Bayon

Dominique Brillaud

WINNING THAT FIRST CLIENT

"When we told prospective clients in Chile that we were a French food services company, people understood what we were about and expressed interest in working with us. French food enjoyed a good reputation among the locals," recalls Dominique Brillaud. "But then the client would inevitably ask to see what we could do. The problem was that we didn't have anything to show because we were just getting started!

"Every day, our team had lunch in a small local restaurant, where we eventually became friends with the owner. One day he said, 'I'd be happy to lend you my kitchen so you can show potential clients what you can do.' So that's what we did, and it allowed us to win our first contract!"

being 7,500 miles away from home, but after a while, you end up learning how to get things done on your own, and that includes grasping the nuances of a country's labor laws and its commercial legislation. The hardest, most complicated part of it all was signing our first client." But through perseverance and team spirit, Sodexho's employees in Chile signed their first contracts, which were to be followed by many others.

At the same time, the company continued to develop its operations in Europe, where it would encounter a mixed fate. Sodexho would follow up on its successes in Italy with attempts to enter the Spanish market in 1975, the year of General Franco's death. It would take five years for the subsidiary to realize its first profits due to the country's unstable political situation as it transitioned to a democratic regime and then experienced a major economic crisis brought on by increasing oil prices.

Growth in the vast German market, where a number of powerful competitors – including Eurest, American leader Aramark and Jacques Borel – had already established themselves, would also prove more difficult than Sodexho had foreseen. But the biggest competition came from local caterers, or *"pächter,"* who offered unbeatable conditions to their clients. Given that 75% of food services offerings were developed in-house and *pächter* held nearly one-quarter of the market, food services providers in Germany were actually fighting over less than 1.5% of the market. Despite a few prestigious clients, including the Max Planck Institute in Stuttgart and Siemens's Frankfurt offices, Sodexho was faced with ongoing losses. The company decided to end its German food services business in 1981, yet maintained a presence in the market through its 1980 acquisition of the meal voucher company DRS, allowing it to pursue growth in a new arena.

With visions of conquering fresh frontiers, Sodexho expanded to more distant lands, such as Australia, where it set up a subsidiary in 1980, and Tahiti, where it had had a presence since 1979. Sodexho's long-standing client, the French Atomic Energy Commission, also asked the company to handle food and hotel-management services for its experimental laboratory in the Pacific. Two years later, Sodexho would sign its first school food services contract in Papeete, the capital of Tahiti and French Polynesia.

Following Dr. Winchendron's Lead

Even though the oil trade was facilitating the company's growth in many ways, Sodexho's senior executives remained fully aware that this source of wealth would one day dry up. They started looking at the meal voucher industry in 1975 as a way to diversify the company's activities.

An English invention, meal vouchers had crossed the Channel in 1957 but would not be offered by specialized companies in France until the early 1960s. In 1962 a banker, Mr. Roger-Vasselin, launched his Chèque-Restaurant meal voucher business, followed by Jacques Borel's Ticket Restaurant company in 1963 and the Chèque Coopératif Restaurant company's Chèque Déjeuner venture in 1964. A lack of regulations favoring the system made for a rough start; the market would not take off until September 27, 1967, when a French ruling formally designated meal vouchers as an employee benefit, affording tax and other exemptions to companies that provided them. The ruling ended up serving employees as much as employers, for it turned meal vouchers into a widely accepted means of paying for the midday meal.

THE FIRST MEAL VOUCHERS

Meal vouchers were first seen in London immediately after the war. A director of a London hospital, Dr. Winchendron, had developed the idea of giving coupons to his employees that they could use to lunch at local restaurants with which the hospital had signed an agreement. The concept soon caught on and would be developed on a large scale by John Hack, founder of Luncheon Vouchers, who, while having lunch with his friends, noticed that certain clients were paying for their meals with coupons. Curious, he asked a waiter about the coupons and was told that the restaurant had agreed to allow employees of certain companies to pay for their meals with vouchers, which were then sent back to the companies for reimbursement.

John Hack realized that the system might interest numerous companies seeking to provide meals for their employees without having to offer in-house cafeteria services. After studying the idea carefully, he and a friend decided to set up a company that would handle all aspects of the service and its logistics in exchange for a commission from clients.

Luncheon Vouchers, or "LVs," were thus launched in 1954, thanks to a 1949 statute granting tax and other exemptions of up to 15 pence per day of work to British companies providing meals to their employees. Two years after its creation, Luncheon Vouchers was acquired by a consortium of nine of the biggest food services and food supply companies in the U.K. John Hack would continue to head the business until his tragic death in a car accident in 1977.

Once this legal framework was in place, the three French meal voucher companies created the CRT association to monitor and reimburse meal vouchers. With the adoption of the meal voucher system by major French banks, these companies were able to expand operations and would soon realize their first profits. "The system is spectacularly successful, especially in the Paris region, and the number of meal vouchers will exceed 100 million a year in 1975," stated business magazine *L'Usine Nouvelle*.

Bellon was watching the early attempts and gradual development of the French meal voucher market with keen interest. As early as 1975, during one of the Board's regular strategy seminars held at the prestigious Abbaye de Royaumont north of Paris, he introduced the idea of meal vouchers and explained how the system worked, its strategic value, and what Jacques Borel had made of it.

Meal vouchers were a natural complement to food services, and they were characterized by a favorable financial model and significantly higher level of profitability than food services. They were most attractive to Sodexho at a time when it was searching for lucrative ways to finance its tremendous growth while reinforcing its reputation and position on the market for providing meals outside the home.

Convinced of the sector's potential, Bellon knew he needed to act quickly and began his search for a partner. In 1976, Sodexho took its first steps in the meal voucher market by founding an association with the Crédit Lyonnais bank in France and acquiring 80% of the Belgian subsidiary of French player Chèque-Restaurant from Roger-Vasselin. Sodexho would face many challenges in the French market, given the three existing players' solid positions and more than ten years' experience – Jacques Borel alone held 44% of the French market. Without significant investment, it would be impossible for Sodexho to penetrate the market, so Sodexho decided to make its first foray into the meal voucher business in Belgium.

Sodexho was facing many challenges in Belgium as it learned about business there the hard way, losing market share and dealing with problems such as voucher forgery. But despite these difficulties, the company would benefit from its beginnings in a new sector of activity.

Sodexho's early attempts to enter the Brazilian market were thwarted by lobbying efforts initiated by Jacques Borel to limit the number of meal voucher companies. It was not until the early 1980s – when Sodexho launched its meal vouchers in France and put in place a fully dedicated team – that the operation

Pierre Henry

took off. It would prove to be a worthwhile journey, however, for the company was soon ranked number two worldwide.

A Natural Complement to Food Services

One of the steps Sodexho took to create the necessary organizational structure for its meal voucher operations was to hire Pierre Henry, now group COO and CEO, Service Voucher and Card operations, as sales manager for Belgium in 1980.

In 1981, Sodexho and the Crédit Lyonnais mutually agreed to end their partnership. Ready to fend for itself, Sodexho concentrated on the French market, where the situation had become clearer. When an opportunity arose to acquire the fourth-ranked Ticket-Repas company, Sodexho did not hesitate to act and immediately worked to make the newly acquired company profitable. It defined a new client-focused sales approach, carried out the all-important task of modernizing the company's image and implemented strict management policies with the goal of lowering costs. Sodexho was rewarded for its efforts, as Ticket-Repas was profitable in fiscal year 1982,

Ticket-Repas: one of the first meal vouchers in France

with a 15% increase in the number of meal vouchers issued compared to an average increase of 5% for the rest of the market.

In 1982, Sodexho created an international service voucher division directed by Albert George. The company had learned from experience that it would not be able to pursue its ambitions in the meal voucher arena without a precise strategy and properly dedicated resources. Until that time, meal vouchers had been part of the food services segment, and the business was often perceived – even by those who were charged with developing it – as conflicting with the interests of food services, hindering the drive for growth.

When Albert George assumed the business, his mission was simple: to catch up to Ticket Restaurant – which ranked first worldwide with operations in eight countries – as quickly as possible. Once again, Sodexho had to face the enormous challenge of trying to outrun the market leader. But its rival had grown weaker, and another, much bigger battle had already begun in which Ticket-Restaurant would not be the smallest stake.

An advertising campaign
for service vouchers in Belgium

7

With Its Head Held High...

Sodexho had come so far since its beginnings: it had overcome many pitfalls standing in the way of its development and embraced the adventures and challenges of its expansion. By the end of the 1970s, it was ranking first in outsourced food services in France and in remote-site management services worldwide. With 14,000 employees working to grow the company on a global scale, Sodexho was earning more than 55% of its revenues outside France and had reached most of the goals it had set for itself.

Despite the company's successes, however, the turbulent 1970s would go out like a lion, not a lamb. To fulfill its founder's global ambitions, Sodexho had to continue to grow, so when an opportunity arose in 1977 to acquire all or part of Jacques Borel International (JBI), which was facing an uncertain future following the resignation of its founder, it seemed like a godsend. But Sodexho would have to deal with competition

"Pierre Bellon builds; he is not a speculator."

from Novotel, a French hotel group whose founders Gérard Pélisson and Paul Dubrule were already eagerly circling their prey.

Creating a Global Leader in Food Services

Sodexho's historic rival, JBI was one of France's first contract food services providers and the creator of the meal voucher concept. It was founded by Jacques Borel – considered by some to have a huge ego and flamboyant public persona – who had successfully expanded the business through the 1960s and 1970s. By the time it came into play, JBI was continental Europe's leading food services provider, serving more than 100 million customers in six countries, and the world's largest meal voucher issuer by revenue, with operations in France, West Germany, Belgium, Italy, Spain, Brazil and Mexico.

For Borel, however, things began to turn sour in 1975, when he beat out Pélisson and Dubrule to acquire the Sofitel luxury hotel chain. It turned out to be a pyrrhic victory. Not only did he pay too much for the chain in the opinion of many, but he soon stumbled in a series of poor marketing decisions, whose impact was aggravated by his public complaints –

expressed in his usual colorful language – deriding the quality of the acquired assets. These moves were not at all appreciated by the financial institutions that had long controlled JBI's capital, and on May 2, 1977 Borel was forced to resign.

When the JBI Board finally handed over management to a financial executive, Pierre Bellon realized that the company was likely to be broken up and sold in pieces as shareholders sought to maximize their financial return rather than pursue a strategic vision for the business. In 1977, therefore, he initiated discussions with Novotel, JBI's leading competitor in the hotel business. He and Rémi Baudin met with Dubrule and Pélisson for the first time at the Mercure hotel near the Porte d'Orléans in Paris. In subsequent meetings, each held in a different location to keep the talks secret, the four men hammered out an offer that would keep the assets in French hands if the JBI Board started looking for buyers. Novotel would acquire the hotels, commercial restaurants and SCAPA purchasing agency, while Sodexho would get the food services and Ticket-Restaurant meal voucher businesses.

For Bellon, it was clear that JBI offered a strong strategic fit with Sodexho and that combining the two would propel an entirely French-owned company to the forefront of the global food services market and create an uncontested leader in meal vouchers. However, this vision was gradually being undermined by other influential voices among the Paris financial establishment, as well as by Pélisson and Dubrule's growing realization that the meal voucher business could provide a valuable source of cash flow for a hotel group.

The first signs of an alternative scenario emerged in June 1980, when the JBI Board decided to sell its Belgian food services division to Aramark. At the same time, French retailing chain Codec-Una acquired a more than 12% stake in JBI, with a seat on the Board. During the summer, JBI then sold Sofitel to Novotel, enabling Pélisson and Dubrule to get their hands on France's leading luxury hotel chain and get themselves into the good graces of JBI's Board.

For Bellon, however, the real shock came in the fall, when the press announced that, at the request of the banks controlling the majority of votes on the Board, JBI's management had been turned over to Pélisson and Dubrule. Without spending a centime or buying a single share, the two men had single-handedly taken command of the company, effectively scuttling the planned joint offer with Sodexho. But Bellon, convinced that his project made better business sense and anxious to prevent any more pieces of the company from being sold to foreigners, persistently spent the next year negotiating an option to acquire JBI's food services and Ticket-Restaurant businesses. The parties were unable to reach an agreement, however, and by January 1982, the process seemed to have come to a close.

Still, Bellon refused to give up, this time trying a different tack. He understood that the only hope of saving his project was to gain a seat on JBI's Board of Directors. In the spring of 1982, Sodexho quietly began buying up JBI shares, building a stake until it reached the 10% it was legally required to publicly disclose.

During the disclosure press conference, Bellon publicly discussed his project for the first time, being sure to remind Dubrule and Pélisson of their previous conversations: "Thanks to your dedication," he said, "Novotel is now the world's ninth-largest hotel chain. I admire your talent as managers and, as you know, hold you both in high esteem. From the meetings we have held about four times a year since 1977 to talk about JBI, you also know that I see major potential for synergy between our two companies. We last met in January. You are familiar with my strategies and my ideas about JBI's development. They have not changed."

> ## Monsieur X,
> ## que voulez-vous faire du groupe Jacques Borel International?
>
> En pleine agitation boursière, les cadres du groupe Jacques Borel International s'adressent à ceux qui remettent en cause le projet d'entreprise.

A June 3, 1982 headline in *Le Figaro* reads, "Mr. X, what are you planning to do with Jacques Borel International?"

A June 7, 1982 headline in *Le Monde* reads, "When Mr. X unmasks himself"

With a special meeting of JBI shareholders called to approve a proposed merger with Novotel on June 28, Bellon's announcement placed Dubrule and Pélisson in a delicate position. In addition, aware of the decisive role Codec-Una would play in JBI's future, Bellon had signed a right-of-first-refusal agreement several weeks earlier with Michel Régnier, the company's CEO. Initiated by bankers at Lazard, the agreement stated that neither Sodexho nor Codec-Una would sell their shares in JBI to a third party without first offering them to one another. As the JBI shareholders prepared to meet, Régnier announced that Codec-Una, which now owned around 27% of JBI's shares, was opposed to the merger.

Novotel's response was not long in coming. Faced with Bellon's proposed merger and the opposition of a significant number of shareholders to the rival JBI-Novotel merger, Pélisson and Dubrule decided to change strategy and make a public offer to purchase JBI in exchange for Novotel shares.

During the doldrums of the Paris summer, each party prepared itself for battle. Sodexho made a counter-offer, causing trading in JBI shares to be suspended. But stock exchange authorities declared the bid inadmissible after the Finance Minister asked the Fair

WHY HAS SODEXHO ACQUIRED 10% OF JBI'S CAPITAL?

"Our two companies are engaged in nearly the same activities and we believe that it is better to work with, rather than against, a major competitor. This seems like a simple, obvious fact to me. I never would have imagined that, within a few days, this transaction would trigger such emotional, passionate responses, which seem somewhat excessive to me ... We cannot sacrifice the long-term future of our companies by refusing to consider a common ground for JBI and Sodexho simply because we don't feel like it ... JBI and Sodexho are involved in the same sectors, with complementary positions in international markets, and our collaboration would considerably reinforce the groups' market shares in food services, meal vouchers and remote-site management services in the 35 countries where we have a presence. The new group would become the leader in nearly 30 of the 35 countries where JBI and Sodexho have operations," explained Pierre Bellon during a June 8, 1982 press conference.

Trade Commission to rule on the mergers. In the end, when trading of JBI shares resumed in early August, neither Sodexho nor Novotel was authorized to buy the company's stock, most of which was purchased by a Codec-Una subsidiary.

The last act was played out in the fall. In early October, the Fair Trade Commission authorized Sodexho's offer on the condition that the company

New offer for Jacques Borel Intl.

Jacques Borel International (JBI), the French catering group which is the takeover target of hotels chain Novotel, has received a counterbid from Sodexho

Financial Times, July 14, 1982

Jacques Borel International : feu vert pour Novotel, feu rouge pour Sodexho

An August 2, 1982 headline in *Les Echos* reads, "Jacques Borel International: Green Light for Novotel, Red Light for Sodexho"

sell its Ticket-Repas subsidiary, France's fourth-largest meal voucher issuer, which would have controlled around 40% of the French market post-merger. Over the next few days, Novotel modified its stock-for-stock offer, and on October 7, Régnier informed the JBI Supervisory Board that Codec-Una would tender its JBI shares to the bid. His decision to break the previous spring's agreement with Sodexho irrevocably sealed the fate of the companies involved.

Betrayed by its closest ally and with little hope of success, Sodexho nevertheless made its own public offer to purchase all outstanding JBI shares. At the press conference, Bellon noted that, "Novotel and Sodexho are now entering the home stretch of a marathon begun five months ago. All of you in the media are saying that Sodexho is going to lose, but we believe we can win. Still, I'd like to remind you that the contest is taking place under most unusual circumstances. The managers of the target company also manage Novotel, which is making an all-paper bid that competes with our cash offer. My goal today is to provide you – and the people who will make the final decision – with the most complete, detailed, precise and objective information." He then reviewed Sodexho's vision for the combined company, the consequences of the merger and the impact on jobs.

That very evening, JBI's Supervisory Board recommended that shareholders tender all of their shares to the Novotel offer. For the Sodexho people whose lives had for so many months revolved around press releases, meetings and unexpected developments, the loss left the bitter taste of having been unfairly defeated. Their disappointment was short-lived, however. "It was a bit like David and Goliath," recalls Raphaël Dubrule, company secretary of Bellon SA. "We had spent many a sleepless night, working like crazy in the middle of the August vacation. It was exhilarating. Sodexho had lost but we came out of it with our heads high."

While Bellon acknowledged a certain naiveté on his part, he also recognized that the bankers behind JBI supported Novotel's offer primarily because, as a hotel group, it was going to need a lot of financing. Sodexho, on the other hand, didn't need to finance anything and, most importantly, had no intention of giving up its independence.

The day after the defeat, Bellon sent a letter to Sodexho managers. "Our attempts to merge with JBI may have failed," he wrote, "but we've learned a lot from the experience. Our raised public profile and our new commitments have positioned us to list Sodexho on the Paris Stock Exchange in the very

Pierre Bellon in his
Montigny-le-Bretonneux office

near future. We should also recognize that there are strategic lessons to be learned. That's why I plan to set up manager meetings in November to explain how the bid took place, answer your questions and talk about the future."

Everyone was also aware that Accor, the new hospitality group created from the merger of JBI and Novotel, was bound to cross paths with Sodexho again.

Sodexho Goes Public

Clodine Pincemin

"When we were first listed on the Paris Stock Exchange," recalls Clodine Pincemin, head of communications at the time and now group executive vice president, Communications and Sustainable Development, "Our phone started ringing off the hook! We received many phone calls from journalists who wanted to visit our factories. Everyone seemed convinced that we supplied companies around the world from giant factories!" That is how little was known about Sodexho and food services in general in the early 1980s.

Sodexho's experience with JBI and its listing on the Paris Stock Exchange garnered more attention for the company than had ten years of growth in various markets and the millions of meals it had served the world over.

"The day Sodexho was listed," reported financial newspaper *Investir* on March 2, 1983, "the company received orders for more than a million shares, worth three times the company's capital! 52,095 shares were finally sold at the price of 230.20 euros, a reasonable price given the frenzy surrounding the newly listed entity. To respond to demand, the company was forced to limit sales to one share per 20 ordered." Five days later, Sodexho's stock price had risen to 269.10 euros.

It had taken a good deal of preparation for Sodexho to be listed on the stock market; as early as 1972, at the behest of Bellon, a committee had been created within the company's financial department to analyze and evaluate the best means of preparing Sodexho to go public and allowing employees to become shareholders. "We had four main objectives," explains Bernard Carton, former group chief financial officer. "We were looking to improve the company's image and awareness among potential and existing clients, suppliers, employees and investors; to allow our employees to purchase stock under advantageous conditions and use stock options as incentives; to

"To improve working conditions, we must address the expectations of our employees while constantly improving our competitiveness."

allow Pierre Bellon's brother and sisters to sell a part of their holdings should they so wish; and, finally, to locate and grow the financial resources that would guarantee external growth for the company."

As the group's companies were being reorganized and its legal and accounting departments were preparing for its listing on the stock market – which would make Sodexho the first European food services company to be listed – its first employee shareholding plan was also being developed. In 1976, 82 of the 150 managers with more than two years' seniority to whom the plan was proposed purchased shares at the bargain price of 15.55 euros per share, which represented only 110% of net assets. They also benefited from 25% vesting per year over the first four years and immediate dividend rights, as well as an ongoing buyback guarantee from Félix Bellon S.A. at the price of purchase plus 12% interest per year.

In the fall of 1982, a few months before the company went public, Pierre Bellon and his family offered shares to 500 additional employees, of which just slightly more than one-third purchased shares, at a price of 114.34 euros per share.

After Sodexho was listed on the stock market, Mireille Mantion, who joined the group in 1970 as a switchboard operator and today serves as head receptionist, went to see Bellon. "It's wonderful that you have made it possible for Sodexho managers to purchase shares under very advantageous conditions," she said, "but what about the people who aren't in management positions? We didn't get anything!"

Pierre Bellon consulted with other Board members, including his brother and sisters, on the matter before deciding to give away three shares to each employee with ten years' seniority, despite concerns that the group's legal and financial advisers expressed for the Bellon family. But Bellon felt strongly about the subject and went ahead, declaring himself ready to publicly defend his offer should financial authorities attempt to overturn it. "I would have loved to go to jail for that. Can you imagine the newspaper headlines? 'Boss goes to jail for giving shares to his employees.'"

This "hand-out," also known as "Operation Dada," did indeed take place, making happy shareholders of 543 employees.

"Going public was an incredible experience for us," remarks Clodine Pincemin, group executive vice president, Communications and Sustainable Development. "We worked intensively with bankers and legal advisors for almost a year. No one was really ready for such an extraordinary experience and we had a great

"We have the right to make mistakes as long as we learn from them."

AN ONGOING COMMITMENT

From the moment he joined the CJP in 1958, Pierre Bellon remained dedicated to causes that went beyond the scope of his company. He spent a great deal of time fighting for the notion of socially responsible companies that adopt and respect a social agenda, as well as for the recognition of food services and the service industry in general, which he felt to be undervalued.

After the CJP, later renamed the CJD, Bellon joined the Economic and Social Council, France's third constitutional assembly, whose responsibilities include issuing recommendations to the French authorities and taking part in the legislative process concerning bills to be submitted to the French parliament. He subsequently joined the CNPF in 1973 as a member of its Social Commission. Ten years later, he was elected vice chairman, a position he still holds today at the CNPF's successor, the MEDEF.

Bellon also contributed a great deal to the creation of organized labor groups representing the food services sector in France, and the SNC (the equivalent of the National Restaurant Association in the U.S. and the British Hospitality Association in the U.K.), which brought together hotel chains, restaurants and food services companies.

In 1983, the SNRC (equivalent of the Food & Service Management Forum in the U.K.) was created from the food services branch of the SNC. That same year, after a series of long negotiations, the first national labor agreement for employees of food services companies in France was signed.

deal to learn as we moved forward. Within the company, we dedicated masses of resources to communicating with our employees; we even implemented a dedicated toll-free hotline. But as employee shareholding was much less common than it is today, only a small number of employees dared to take the risk."

The spring of 1983 would mark a turning point in Sodexho's history. In a speech before the company's Annual Shareholders' Meeting on February 25, 1983, Bellon declared, "We are enjoying growth inside and outside of France. With average annual increases of 33% in business volume and 50% in profits, our results are beyond satisfactory. To safeguard our growth, we must sometimes take risks. We often succeed, but sometimes we do not – our most recent failure being Sodexho's much-documented attempt to merge with Jacques Borel International. However, we feel that we have the right to make mistakes as long as we learn from them."

Now one of the big players, Sodexho would be operating under the watchful eyes of financial analysts. After being nurtured and shaped under the Marseilles sun, the start-up was approaching the beginning of a real revolution.

Second Era: 1970–1983

The importance
of employees

*

Pursuit of growth drivers

*

A local hiring policy

*

Financial management
of development

During this period, Sodexho's revenues grew by a factor of 79, from 6.5 to 511.5 million euros, at an average annual growth rate of 40%. Net income increased by a factor of 109, from 120,000 euros to 13.1 million euros at an average annual growth rate of 43%.

Third Era (1984–1994)

A DECADE OF CHANGE

"Thanks to a rate of success that slightly outpaced our setbacks, Sodexho grew by leaps and bounds."

Always ready to anticipate shifts in market forces and trail-blaze new initiatives, in the mid-1980s Sodexho adopted a segmented approach to meet the market changes it foresaw. It was also time for the group to take on the challenge of the world's biggest market: the U.S. Sodexho would prove its mettle by becoming the first French food services company to launch operations in the U.S.

As Sodexho's activities spread around the globe, Pierre Bellon grew more and more convinced that the group would have to join forces with another company if it wanted to reinforce its position in its markets and outdistance the increasingly intense competition. In 1989, Sodexho teamed up with the venerable Compagnie Internationale des Wagons-Lits (CIWLT) and its food services subsidiary, Eurest. The short-lived joint venture would be a tough blow that would test Sodexho's capacity to learn and rebound from setbacks. Within months, however, the fiercely independent Sodexho would do just that, demonstrating again the primary quality of an entrepreneur as it re-intensified its efforts to become a global leader in food services. This focus on international development paid off: between 1990 and 1994, the group launched operations in 25 new countries.

8

_ Beyond Our Wildest Dreams _

With a presence in 42 countries, Sodexho clearly had what it would take to continue its growth. Its entrepreneurial, decentralized culture, ongoing commitment to strict management policies and global vision allowed the group to remain highly flexible in adapting to local market conditions. This critical business element of flexibility would prove to be a serious competitive advantage in the group's expansion.

Market forces were at work and food services was no longer a new market in which providers were trying to build a foundation for new client offerings. This was especially true in France, which contributed 42% of Sodexho's revenues in fiscal year 1983. The group's competition was increasing, and each competitor had learned valuable lessons. "I am amazed by the diversity and quality of offerings on the French market," stated one of Sodexho's international competitors. "They go way beyond what we are seeing in other markets." Ahead of its European counterparts,

"We must be there when opportunities arise and rapidly adapt our resources to changing economic conditions."

the French market – led by Sodexho, Générale de Restauration and Eurest – had seen the rise of many new players, often local or specialized. Customers had access to an increasingly diverse range of services that had little in common with the first food services offered to the canteens of 20 years earlier.

Customers were more aware of their options and more demanding than ever, especially with the rise of the restaurant industry's alternative approaches to inexpensive fast food. Following the long-prevailing model of the U.S. market, competition was popping up on every block.

Blossoming creative marketing approaches had led to deep-seated change in the way companies related to their clients, as they sought to grow closer to them and adapt services to their needs.

"It is no longer simply a question of feeding our customers or making sure our cafeterias are running smoothly. Nearly all of our competitors can do that. To get ahead and have a true competitive edge, we need to offer a distinctive level of quality in our services, as well as varied, original menus," summed up Rémi Baudin, senior executive vice-president of Sodexho at the time. Meanwhile, to compensate for declines in the remote-site management industry, Sodexho intensified its efforts abroad and launched its strategy to dominate the world's biggest market, the U.S.

Dedication to Clients

In a presentation of the group's results to journalists on October 30, 1984, Pierre Bellon summed up his view of how Sodexho would have to adapt. "In prehistoric times, dinosaurs and ants lived peacefully together. As the world around them evolved, it became increasingly difficult for the mammoth dinosaur to satisfy its needs, and all species of dinosaur would eventually disappear from the Earth forever. Only the industrious, organized, disciplined and flexible ant managed to survive, even to this day, thanks to its ability to adapt to the changing face of its natural environment.

"With 8,130 employees and 840 sites in France, Sodexho has become a dinosaur. As an industry heavyweight, we have to intensify our efforts to compensate for the weight of our success, history and size.

"To get closer to our clients, allow our employees to take on more responsibility, accelerate growth, and leverage our size without losing sight of what it means to be a small company and the benefits we derive

"Keep the advantages of a big company while retaining the benefits of a small business."

"Segmentation would prove to be a key weapon in the group's strategy."

from that, we have decided to divide our business into three client segments: business & industry, healthcare and education.

"These specialized, more competent divisions will allow us to act as true partners where our clients are concerned."

At that moment, Bellon's metaphor of the dinosaur and the ant was most unexpected. The resilient leader revealed that, despite Sodexho having barely recovered from the unfortunate JBI incident, he was ready to place a serious bet on the group's future by implementing a visionary approach.

Bellon realized that the industry in which his group had set the pace for nearly 20 years was about to undergo a service revolution. Thanks to technological advances in the food industry and the modernization of food processing equipment, companies like Sodexho were now able to focus their employees' attention on developing new techniques and services. Those preparing the food could now move away from the more mundane aspects of food preparation and focus on the quality of service. "The future of the food services industry," summed up Bellon, "lies in making the corporate dining hall experience resemble a restaurant experience. The clients in both outlets are the same and they have the same demands."

THE RESTAURANT INDUSTRY:
A TESTING GROUND FOR FOOD SERVICES

The creation of the *Oh! Poivrier* restaurant chain in 1985 would mark one of Sodexho's rare forays into the commercial restaurant world. "*Oh! Poivrier* was the result of close collaboration between Patrick Derdérian and Pierre Bellon. The experiment was driven by the former's creative talent and the latter's conviction that food services needed to draw upon the expertise of the restaurant sector, especially in terms of marketing," explains Didier Chenet, who took over management of the chain in 1990. "There was no question about it: Bellon fully realized the need to understand consumer expectations."

The experience allowed Bellon to realize his dream of offering quality fast food while respecting French culinary standards. Based on an original concept – an entire meal served on a single plate – the *Oh! Poivrier* chain first opened its doors in March 1985 on Avenue du Maine in Paris. The restaurant's interior was decorated in shades of gray "to contrast with the colorful meals." All in all, nine branches would open in Paris by 1990.

After an unsuccessful attempt to launch the chain in London, Chenet, along with a number of fellow managers, executed a management buyout in 1993. "*Oh! Poivrier* provided a true testing ground for Pierre Bellon," states Chenet, now president and CEO of the chain. To this day, the *Oh! Poivrier* adventure continues, with a modernized concept that appeals to today's consumers.

Didier Chenet

In 1984, the education sector accounted for 8% of Sodexho's revenues in France

For the group to satisfy the expectations of a new generation of clients, it would have to focus its resources on a single goal: listening to clients and understanding their needs. Segmenting the group's businesses into divisions would prove to be an ingenious step and one of Sodexho's crowning strategic moves, as it faced up to many difficult challenges and reaped equally significant rewards. The segmented approach allowed Sodexho to become the leader in the healthcare market, first in France and then worldwide, and 20 years later it would remain a spearhead of the group's sales strategy and play a key role in balancing risk in its client portfolio.

While segmentation was a relatively simple process – allocate specialized resources to different client segments to more effectively address their needs – it represented a profound and somewhat wrenching shift for a company that had always been organized by geographic market. In addition, corporate clients accounted for 46% of consolidated revenues at the time, whereas education generated only 8% and healthcare 11%.

"We took a risk in segmenting our business," underscores Baudin. "In France, for example, we were dealing with a limited number of healthcare clients and had not reached the critical mass that would have warranted a dedicated organizational structure, with the ensuing costs."

The new organization forced each segment to rethink its way of doing business to meet new challenges. Both the healthcare and education divisions had to build a wider client base, but the business & industry division, the group's first line of business, was confronted with the equally difficult issues of increasingly entrenched competition and slowing demand for outsourced services.

In fact, the group would see the most outstanding results in its healthcare division, which benefited the most from the segmented approach. Sodexho's pursuit of hospitals, clinics and homes for seniors was driven by the entrepreneurial spirit at the heart of the group's values.

"Just before the new divisions were created," recalls Jean-Michel Dhenain, who was put in charge of the healthcare business, "Pierre Bellon asked me to look at what the U.S. competition was doing. I spent three months visiting different sites and cafeterias, and meeting with players such as Saga, Canteen Corp, Marriott and Aramark. I also talked to many journalists and investors in the sector."

Sodexho: attentive to patient needs

A Sodexho Healthcare patient liaison officer

Dhenain returned to France convinced of one thing: in order to succeed, Sodexho would have to go beyond the kitchen to create a complete services offering for its healthcare and senior clients. This would mark a serious break with the group's traditional approach.

"In the healthcare sector, we could no longer think of ourselves as food services providers only. We had to go beyond the traditional separation of services, which detracted from service quality and decreased our teams' motivation," says Dhenain. "We needed to get to know the patients we were serving and play a role in the services and the environment with which we were working. After visiting companies in the U.S. that worked this way, I told Pierre Bellon and Rémi Baudin that there was no reason why we could not take the same approach to help us differentiate our group from the other players in the French market. We began with a small team and started to rebuild the business from scratch, as we had at the very beginning of the group's history."

"We were true pioneers," recalls Yann Coléou, who joined the healthcare sales team in 1985 and is now president, Food and Management Services France.

"Potential clients had no idea what the food services business was all about; they had no idea that such services existed."

Sodexho developed a new offering that included meals for patients and employees, meal distribution, housekeeping and other residential services. The group positioned itself as a full-service partner with healthcare institutions and began conducting customer satisfaction surveys on a regular basis. After being tested in Nancy, Sodexho rolled out its Site Liaison Officer concept to ensure smooth relations between healthcare professionals, food services staff and housekeeping, and to verify that patient needs were being met.

Full of enthusiasm and confident about its approach, the young team was not disappointed by the results. In fiscal year 1987, the group's healthcare division contributed 18.4% of revenues in France.

Sodexho's healthcare division was not the only pioneer in its sector; the group's education division was trailblazing a new approach to the market. "Having specialized divisions allows us to intimately familiarize ourselves with the expectations of our various customers," said the head of the division at the time. "In nursery and elementary schools, providing balanced meals is of utmost importance, whereas junior high and high school students value their lunchtime as

Educating children on nutrition

A chef and site manager
taste an appetizing dish
created using the freshest products

a break in a busy day. For the latter, our role is not only nutritional; we must also concern ourselves with the environment in which the meals we prepare are being served." Using state-of-the-art central kitchens that featured the latest developments in the food industry, especially where fresh products, raw products and prepared, ready-to-use items were concerned, and new technologies, including vacuum-packed cooking techniques, the division was able to provide higher-quality, more diverse services and free up its employees to focus on the notion of service and the well-being of customers.

The changes implemented in 1984 would lead to a completely new approach to educational food services a few years later: the education division would team up with researchers to teach children how to eat more balanced, healthy meals without taking away from their fun at mealtime, where they interacted with their classmates. This revolutionary approach would begin with the "Helping You Grow" educational program.

An Eye on Innovation

Along with reorganizing food and management services according to client segments, the group also created a quality department in France that embodied the training and development objectives Pierre Bellon had held dear from the beginning. "We are already committed to teaching, training and motivating our teams, but we would like to go even further," Bellon stated. "We realize that employees represent a potential goldmine of innovation and creativity."

When a company chooses to rely on organic growth, innovation is key to maintaining leadership over the long haul. In an increasingly competitive French market, the group preserved an intense focus on continually providing value for clients and Bellon's conviction was confirmed. "Constant progress is our only means of differentiating ourselves from the competition," he told his colleagues. "This alone will enable us to show our clients and customers that our services evolve to match their changing needs and that we are constantly improving our offering." In 1986, Michel Dubois, head of Strategic Planning, Innovation and Quality, asked Alain Neyrinck, who was until then in charge of developing the remote-site business, to oversee the group's innovation department. "Working with Alain, we spent months thinking about where we needed to go, gathering information and trying to understand and define the notion of innovation and its ramifications for a group like Sodexho," recounts Dubois. "We came up with an

Michel Dubois

Alain Neyrinck

The closing ceremony
of the World Innovation Forum
in Marseilles, 2002

innovation process that could be pursued at the group level. It wasn't very long before we recognized that we should find out about the innovative approaches being developed in the group's various subsidiaries to leverage them throughout the organization." This realization would lead to the creation of the Sodexho World Innovation Forum, which first took place in 1989.

Sodexho celebrated its 20th anniversary in 1986. It had enjoyed unforeseen success and counted more than 30,000 employees in 40 countries a mere two decades after its creation. The group had stayed true to the path of international development that its founder had chosen after receiving that decisive phone call from American businessman Bill Fishman.

Organic growth had played an important role in the group's development from its very inception. The same year that Sodexho celebrated its 20th anniversary, Pierre Bellon formalized organic growth as part of the group's corporate vision for the first time in its history. "Outlining a group's corporate vision was a relatively new approach," underscores Bellon. "Today, it may be a common management tool, but at the time, few companies worked this way. I was always convinced – and continue to be so – that in order to run a company, concrete reference points and direction were required by the group's employees. They needed to know where we were headed and where we wanted to go. The bigger the group got, the more these elements had to be formalized, disseminated and communicated at all levels. This was the reasoning behind our corporate vision statement in 1986, an approach that would become common practice within the group."

The corporate vision statement was presented to top management during an international seminar held in Paris. The rest of the group's employees would learn about it via a range of internal communications initiatives, including a video that would be shown in all of Sodexho's markets. Drawing on the symbolism of the sea and the shipping industry, the corporate vision statement alluded to the early days of the group as it defined its goals for the future and reminded its audience of the principles that should guide their daily performance.

While the group's philosophy remained faithful in every way to the vision embraced by Pierre Bellon when he created Sodexho, its scope had multiplied. The group's corporate vision statement read, "We now rank sixth worldwide, after five American and British companies. Our goal is to rank first, second or third within the next ten years." It was the first time

"This corporate vision statement provides the alignment we absolutely must have for the group to be effective. It guides us in our strategic planning, daily actions and the decision-making process at all levels of the organization."

The group formalizes its corporate vision in 1986

In daily contact with customers

that the group had openly declared its desire to become "one of the leading global players in the out-sourced food services industry." This objective would influence every major decision facing the group and its founder in the years to come.

To successfully deploy this corporate vision and make it a reality, Bellon chose eight drivers – Profit, Growth, Clients and Customers, Entrepreneurs, People, Organization, Innovation and Communications – that reflected the culture of service and progress which Bellon and his executive team had long sought to instill in the organization.

After many ups and downs, especially for the business & industry division, and an investment of 45.7 million euros, the segmentation of the group's activities in France finally paid off in 1987. "Follow-ing a massive transformation, Sodexho was once again enjoying long-term growth." The press was well-disposed toward the group's turnaround, reporting, "Sodexho saw 31% growth at constant exchange rates in its consolidated net income, over three times the 10% increase predicted by financial analysts for fiscal year 1987." With consolidated net income of 14.5 million euros, Sodexho saw its stock price rise 10% to reach 320.14 euros after its financial results were released. Even the financial crisis of the mid-1980s failed to stop the group's progress.

The business & industry division resumed its growth trend in 1988 under the leadership of its new managing director, Teddy Megarbane, who had returned to France after developing the group's food services business in Saudi Arabia. "Our 'Moving Forward Together, Faster than the Competition' initiative allowed us to enter a phase of progress and growth, which helped improve our figures," he recalls. The revival of the subsidiary was also evident in more concrete forms, including a food services contract for Bouygues's state-of-the-art Challenger headquarters, located in Saint-Quentin-en-Yvelines, southwest of Paris.

The group demonstrated an unprecedented level of professionalism and the ability to create specialized offerings during this phase of its development. It would develop different types and ranges of menus, dishes, services and prices, while implementing management training and executive marketing programs to improve quality and client and customer satisfaction. Sodexho's teams were thus able to overcome the challenges of the group's first real bout of growing pains.

Teddy Megarbane

Sodexho France business & industry segment initiative: "Developing team spirit, showcasing the contribution of each member and moving forward faster than the competition."

Sodexho acquires Bateaux Parisiens
in 1987

Nathalie Szabo

It was also at this time that the group sought to restore balance among its food services activities to compensate for a downturn in the remote-site market, which had accounted for two-thirds of the group's profits as recently as fiscal year 1984. Sodexho would begin testing the waters in new market sectors to see where diversification might prove successful.

The group launched its leisure services business in 1987 with the acquisition of Bateaux Parisiens and its nine cruise ships on the Seine River. The adventure began quite simply: one of Bellon's bankers asked if Sodexho might be interested in acquiring a cruise ship business on the Seine and Bellon once again made a sound business decision simply by listening to his heart. As passionate as ever about the sea and the shipping industry, the entrepreneur was instantly sold on the idea. He asked Bernard Carton, at that time group chief financial officer, to study the possibility of acquiring Bateaux Parisiens and took his wife and children to try one of its cruises along the Seine. This was common practice for the entrepreneur, who rarely missed an opportunity to try out a new restaurant or restaurant concept, as his daughter, Nathalie Szabo, managing director of Sodexho Prestige in France, points out: "My father is an excellent food critic. When we were little, he took us to try all the latest restaurants. He would chat with the owners and get answers to all of his questions. He instilled in me a passion for the restaurant industry at a very early age." This time was no exception, and at the end of the cruise Bellon had made up his mind: "The views are magnificent, but the food served is mediocre at best; we cannot but improve on the services being offered."

Despite lackluster food services, Bateaux Parisiens, with its prestigious location at the foot of the Eiffel Tower, was profitable. Although the river cruise business would require the group to invest in cruise ships, something that went against its guiding principle of avoiding markets that required capital-intensive investments, it offered an attractive financial model in that it generated a great deal of cash. And cruises on the Seine would complement the other services the group offered to its various clients while also adding to the company's positive image. After a few months of negotiations, a deal was signed on June 27, 1987 and Bateaux Parisiens officially became part of the group.

Sodexho's acquisition of Bateaux Parisiens would prove to be a stroke of genius; the company's sales increased six-fold over the next 15 years and, drawing upon the body of expertise developed in its core business, Sodexho would make it the seventh most visited

A Bateaux Parisiens tour boat at the foot of the Eiffel Tower

A transportation service on the Seine

tourist attraction in France. Rather than resting on its laurels, in 1989 the group would also launch a transportation service on the Seine, the Batobus, in partnership with the Ministry of Transport, the City of Paris and the Paris Port Authority.

Quick to follow up on its initial success in the industry, Sodexho attempted to develop its river and harbor cruise business outside France. The acquisition of Spirit Cruises in the U.S. in 1990-1991 and Bateaux London in 1992, however, would not prove as fruitful as the Bateaux Parisiens model, which would remain an anomaly throughout the group's development in more than one way.

On land, the group would prove less than successful in attempts to expand its leisure services business. Nice's Parc Zygofolies amusement park, in which Sodexho invested in 1986, went bankrupt, and the Smurfland amusement park in eastern France, another project in which it was involved, proved unsuccessful as well. Pierre Bellon would also take an interest in natural spring resorts in the early 1990s when the Chaîne du Soleil group went up for sale, but this operation would also remain outside the group's main lines of business.

In its attempts to expand beyond its core business, Sodexho also faced difficulties in the restaurant industry. The *Oh! Poivrier* chain would find its niche under the management of Didier Chenet, but another partnership with young entrepreneur Patrick Derdérian and his passion for theme restaurants proved less prosperous. The head of the *Amanguier* restaurant and *Framboisier* pastry shop chains in the early 1980s, Derdérian joined forces with Sodexho to develop the concepts abroad, but Sodexho quickly realized that the restaurant business required specific expertise – particularly in real estate – that the group was lacking. Attempts to roll out the *Amanguier* chain in Chicago would prove unsuccessful and the group was unable to launch the *Framboisier* chain in Japan due to the lack of a local investor-partner.

While the group experimented with various approaches in France and elsewhere around the world, however, its American dream was taking shape on the other side of the Atlantic.

The American Dream

Pierre Bellon was convinced that his global ambitions for Sodexho required a presence in North America. Driven by his belief in the potential of the American market and his conviction that it was at least five years ahead of Europe, he asked Jean Frégnac in 1983 to start looking for opportunities in new, fast-growing segments of the American service industry market.

Once again, Bellon's intuition was on the mark. A study carried out for Sodexho by a New York firm identified young companies based on new concepts such as those implemented by FedEx and Kentucky Fried Chicken. More importantly, however, the study revealed that the American food services market, worth 44.48 billion dollars in 1984, was chock-full of growth opportunities – despite a 40% penetration level, one of the highest in the world. An in-depth strategic analysis by two Cornell University professors settled any doubts: the American dream was indeed within Sodexho's reach. The group would first take on the U.S. market in the healthcare sector, where food services were growing fastest.

Of course, it would take a certain amount of guts for Sodexho – worth "only" 0.6 billion euros – to face the leading world players in the food services industry on their own turf. The group once again found itself pitted against the Goliaths of the industry, including ARA Services, provider of food services to the Los Angeles Olympics, with sales of 2.4 billion euros and more than 100,000 employees, and Marriott

Management Services, with sales of 1.8 billion euros. Sodexho would be the first French company to start sniffing out the trail of the American leaders, a risky game in which, thus far, only certain British companies had tried their luck.

But Sodexho knew it would be suicidal to try launching operations in the U.S. from scratch and on its own. So it started looking for a well-run, reputable, profitable company with serious growth potential and an affordable price tag. Two years later in 1985, Sodexho finally found the "gem" it was looking for and promptly acquired 100% of capital in Seiler's, New England's leading food services company.

An independent company like Sodexho, Seiler's was looking to be acquired by a European group rather than an American behemoth. As its president Jay Cochrane and executive vice president Phil Gorman – both shareholders in the company – prepared to retire, they wanted to make sure that the group acquiring Seiler's would continue to pursue the same strategy that had made the company a success and contributed to its positive image. Most importantly, the founders wanted to find someone who would keep the current management team in place.

Seiler's was acquired in 1985

The acquisition of Seiler's made Sodexho the leading French food services company in the U.S. and the fifth-ranked player worldwide. Furthermore, the group's executives had achieved the dual objectives they had set forth in undertaking the "American initiative": it had become a player in the world's biggest market and had found an opportunity with strong growth potential in the U.S. healthcare sector. Seiler's, which had signed its first contracts with the Good Samaritan and Emerson hospitals in 1962[1], was the sixth-ranked food services company in the healthcare sector, which accounted for 60% of its sales.

Seiler's' entry into the group may have been a victory for Sodexho, but it was viewed as anything but by Seiler's employees, who were shaken by the arrival of the French company in New England. Few of the company's executives had known about the acquisition beforehand, and the last thing they expected was to be bought out by a French company no one had ever heard of! The first meeting between Seiler's executive managers, Bellon, Patrice Douce and Carton would go down in the group's history. Seiler's managers may have been relieved to learn that their jobs were safe, as Sodexho had decided to maintain the existing management team, but they remained incredulous. "We made it clear who we were and

---

1. In 2002, Sodexho celebrated the 40th anniversary of these two contracts.

A Decade of Change

DID YOU SAY "LOVERS"?

Scene: An office in Boston.

Time: The early 1980s.

Known for his witty humor and love of language, Pierre Bellon often talked about the perils of communicating across cultures and between languages. He was fond of pointing out the "malentendus" (misunderstandings) that can arise in conversations.

In one such occurrence, which has become part of the company's lore, Bellon and then vice president of finance Bernard Carton were at the negotiating table with Sodexho's team of American lawyers. They were about to begin negotiations for the acquisition of Seiler's with that organization's lawyers and company leaders. The meeting was taking place without translators, because Carton was fluent in English.

The negotiations began. Everything was going smoothly until Bellon felt something had gone amiss. He turned to the table…

Bellon: "My lovers told me…"

Dead silence. Startled, the Americans looked wide-eyed at Bellon.

Bellon: "Yes, my lovers told me…"

Carton *(whispering to* Bellon): "'Lawyers,' monsieur. 'Lawyers,' not 'lovers.'"

After clearing up the misunderstanding and enjoying a good laugh, the group resumed negotiations…

what we wanted to do," explained then senior VP Douce, who moved to Boston in 1987 to run the group's North American operations. "Their biggest fear was that we were going to sell the company. We told them that we wanted to offer the same services in the U.S. that we were delivering in other markets. We

The Calgary Winter Olympics would mark the beginning of an ongoing relationship with the Olympic community. Drawing upon their experience in the remote-site business, Sodexho's Canadian teams provided food services for 600 athletes, 300 coaches and doctors as well as 2,500 reporters over a three-week period.

As the group began familiarizing itself with the great Olympic family, it started to build a body of expertise that would be instrumental in the signing of food services contracts for the Albertville Winter Olympics four years later, followed by the Summer and Paralympic Games in Barcelona.

explained that our goal was to go national and one day overtake the leader in the field. The room stirred. They simply didn't understand what we Frenchmen were doing there!"

During this period of mutual discovery, Bellon's charisma and personality would play a vital role – despite his halting English – in fostering confidence among the employees of Sodexho's new American subsidiary.

From this first vantage point on the east coast, Sodexho continued to expand in the U.S. Its acquisition of California-based Food Dimension Inc. (FDI) would serve as a foothold for the group on the west coast and afford it a number of solid client references in the seniors sector. But for FDI's employees, the news of the acquisition was as great a shock as it had been for those of Seiler's. When Bellon met with them for the first time, he shared his belief that Sodexho would lead the U.S. market within 15 years and, despite the language barrier, managed to communicate his enthusiasm, telling FDI's employees that they were the company's best assets in the pursuit of market leadership.

The following year in 1987, Sodexho acquired Canadian food services and remote-site management company Crawley & McCracken. Founded in 1912, in its early days it specialized in remote-site management and was responsible for feeding railway workers as they endeavored to connect Canada's vast geography by rail.

In Canada, Sodexho was woven out of a rich fabric of 16 companies that came together over the course of 94 years dating back to the founding of Crawley & McCracken. These companies, which ranged in size, geography and services, all made an important contribution to the burgeoning food and management services industry. "Sodexho is now a leader in Canada for food and facilities management, providing services to 300 clients at more than 750 sites," remarks Garry Knox, president and CEO of Sodexho Canada since 1996. A wide array of food and facilities management services (housekeeping, plant operation and maintenance, grounds-keeping and laundry) are delivered to corporate, education, healthcare, government, hotel and remote sites. Operations range from coast to coast, on and offshore, conducted in both of Canada's official languages, English and French.

Sodexho also continued to expand its American network with the acquisition of Michigan food services company Western Food Enterprises that same year. Two small local companies, In Plant and Dietary Consult Inc., joined Sodexho's American subsidiary in 1988.

"Sodexho's culture is also one of confidence."

Garry C. Knox

Michel Landel

By this time, the group was generating 26% of its sales in North America, but it had yet to build a unique brand identity and organizational structure. Replacing Patrice Douce, whose return to France had been requested by Pierre Bellon, the new head of the group's American subsidiary, Michel Landel, would immediately begin to address these issues.

Landel began his Sodexho career in 1984 in the Middle East and Africa, where he was involved in the group's remote-site business, becoming president of the group's African operations in 1986. His personal and professional qualities, as well as his passion for living abroad, made him the perfect candidate to spearhead Sodexho's growth in the North American market.

The task of bringing Seiler's and FDI together and instilling in them the group's culture would prove to be no easy feat, and Landel soon realized that it would be a long process. Not only had the two companies based their success on a strong local identity, but the U.S. food services industry had developed in a different way from its French counterpart. In the U.S., cost–plus contracts[1] were a common practice: "It was a way of working that created a strong culture, with our employees feeling more attached to their clients than to the group that employed them," explains Landel.

1. According to this type of contract, a food services company acts on behalf of its client, who is responsible for paying all bills related to food services plus a commission to the provider. In France, on the other hand, almost all contracts provide for a fixed fee so that food services companies absorb any profits or losses.

A Decade of Change

He would have his work cut out for him in trying to combine this client-oriented culture with the profit and loss-oriented culture that had led to Sodexho's success.

Aware that it would take time to implement such deep-seated changes, Landel made sure Bellon knew that the transition would not be immediate. "To succeed in the U.S.," Landel explains, "we needed to have a long-term vision. I told Pierre Bellon that we would have to be patient, but that we would reap the results in the end. Fortunately, he embraced this long-term vision. There was an ongoing feeling of confidence that inspired me to do what I had to do to get the job done so long as I was acting in good conscience and with intellectual honesty. Sodexho's culture is also one of trust."

Backed by Bellon's support, Landel implemented an ambitious program built around the group's strengths in the area of human resources, leveraging the mobility of its employees, its corporate culture and its dedication to training.

The creation of a unified group and reorganized teams would depend on close collaboration with Sodexho's human resources department.

Former Seiler's employee Jay Marvin was placed at the head of FDI and charged with the mission of building a new strategy for the company. The group

Jay Marvin

An example of promotional materials for the *Tasty Lite Cuisine* program initiated in the 1980s

An example of a *Tasty Lite Cuisine* ad

decided to start hiring people from other sectors in the U.S. to gain their valuable outside perspective for the benefit of teams already in place. Landel had an idea: he drew on the talents and experience of women and men who had demonstrated their value to the group elsewhere, such as in Saudi Arabia, to build the U.S. operations. They would be his leaders during the U.S. integration and he would come to rely on them to spread Sodexho's methods and culture in the new American context. Instilling the corporate culture in the new teams took a great deal of patience and perseverance, but Sodexho's message began to take root in the fertile North American soil.

Training – whether on-the-job, as in markets such as Belgium and the Middle East, or at the recently created Sodexho Management Institute (SMI) – was another crucial factor in successfully integrating the group's new employees into existing teams. "I was a firm believer in the SMI," remarks Landel. "It played a major role in helping us assimilate our new American employees into the group. It wasn't long after I arrived in the U.S. that I realized we would never move forward without drawing upon the experience of the men and women who were behind the success of Seiler's and FDI. I sent them to France to provide opportunities for exchange. More than anything else, we knew

SODEXHO TAKES THE LEAD IN NUTRITION IN THE UNITED STATES

When Sodexho first entered the U.S. market, it soon realized how important nutrition was to its customers. In response, it began developing a variety of initiatives geared toward better nutrition in both knowledge and practice. Today, as an industry leader, it offers its accounts full nutritional support, supplying them with everything from educational programs to recipe analysis and the support resources of regional dietitians.

One way in which Sodexho demonstrates its commitment to customer health is through the *Tasty Lite Cuisine* (TLC) program. Based on the U.S. government's new Dietary Guidelines for Americans, TLC offers dishes prepared with minimal calories, sodium, cholesterol and fat. Working in conjunction with TLC is the *Strides For Life* program, which stresses the benefits of combining a healthy diet with walking and regular exercise, and the *Snap Into Shape* and *Partners in Health* information series, which covers such topics as heart disease, cholesterol levels and the role of fiber, iron and calcium in the diet.

Backed by quality materials, expansion support services and highly trained staff, these programs not only perpetuate good eating habits among customers but also help them reach their personal health goals.

we had to build trust between the American teams and the rest of the group." Trial-and-error was part of the learning process as well: "In the beginning, I tried to change things too quickly, but that error in judgment served a purpose in the end because if I hadn't

SO... SODEXHO

The creation of the organization's American subsidiary was supported by a major communications initiative. Not a recognized name in the U.S., the group used an alliterative approach to build its renown. The repetition of "So, So, So..." was intended to automatically evoke the name Sodexho in the consumer's mind and emphasize the values of the men and women behind its success: "So innovative, So flexible, So diverse, So global, So personal."

With a newly established brand identity, the subsidiary would be able to advertise itself to American clients as an international group with operations in 46 countries.

approached the situation the way I did, Sodexho's American subsidiary would never have undergone such profound change."

To create a common purchasing department for Seiler's and FDI in 1990, Landel summoned a colleague from his days in Saudi Arabia. "This was a priority for me because I was convinced we could improve our purchasing processes," he explains. The unified purchasing system, a model that would soon be copied by the competition, would also help finance Sodexho's U.S. growth.

Last but not least, a third initiative would bring Seiler's and FDI closer together than ever before: they would unite under one name. It was the perfect solution — what better way to forge a common identity for the two teams? In the fall of 1993, the group's American subsidiary, comprising the five companies acquired in the U.S., was officially rebaptized under the Sodexho brand. Michel Landel asked Steve Brady, who had been with the group since 1990 and who today serves as senior vice president, Corporate Communications North America, to spearhead the project. "People really wanted to unite under the banner of a single organization," Brady recalls. "There was a real need for our employees to feel they belonged to the same group, the same family. We needed everyone to know that we were moving in the same direction and to feel proud of that fact. Before our rebranding, our American colleagues would often refer to Sodexho as 'They'; after the name change, they finally began to say 'We.'"

Pierre Bellon and Sodexho learned an important lesson from the difficulties encountered in entering the U.S. market: the successful acquisition of a services company depends solely on employee loyalty, which cannot be bought like factories or equipment.

Sodexho was now poised as France's leading food services provider, with 27% of the market, compared to Générale de Restauration's 22% and Eurest's 17%. Sodexho had also taken a major step in its global ambitions. Now ranked number five worldwide, the group was faced with more challenges than ever before. The sector was undergoing rapid consolidation in the U.S. and Europe, with the latter market made highly attractive by the prospect of a single European market. British company Gardner Merchant, the leader in the U.K. and Europe, caused quite a stir in France when it acquired fourth-ranked SLHR (Société Lyonnaise d'Hôtellerie et de Restauration) and third-ranked Cérès in 1987. "Like any other form of competition," Bellon responded, "this will push us to offer higher-quality services and become more

Steve Brady

The American subsidiary adopted the Sodexho name in 1993

competitive." At the same time, he made no secret of Sodexho's intentions: "To move up in the world rankings, we have to join forces with one of the top ten. In light of the potential synergies, the arrival of the single European market in 1992[1] and just plain common sense, it should be a European company."

1. The year the Maastricht Treaty was signed, providing for the creation of the European Union.

9

If at First
You Don't Succeed...

Things were running smoothly. Sodexho was continuing to expand in Europe while growing its share of the meal voucher market and reinforcing its position as the worldwide leader in remote sites.

Sodexho joined forces with the Compagnie Internationale des Wagons-Lits et du Tourisme (CIWLT) in 1989. Their union would be short-lived, however, with the two companies going their separate ways after only 18 months. Fully independent once again, Sodexho would pull itself together and pursue its growth strategy.

Full Steam Ahead

The first meeting of Sodexho's International Executive Committee on September 27-28, 1988 brought together the heads of the group's main businesses and regions.

One of the first meetings
of the International Executive Committee
in Rome, 1990

The newly formed committee – which would evolve into the present-day Operational Committee – was an important symbol of the group's successful international initiative; the group was earning nearly 65% of its revenues abroad at that point. From this time forward, the International Executive Committee oversaw the implementation of the group's policies around the globe.

From Europe to South America, Sodexho's international network had continued to grow and the group had made it a priority to concurrently develop its food and management services as well as its service voucher and card activities whenever possible.

Spain was no exception. Sodexho had strengthened its position by signing a partnership agreement with a local food services company in 1987. The following year, it launched its first Cheque Restaurante meal vouchers in Madrid and Barcelona. Despite great potential, the market was slow to deliver; it was still common practice for employees to take a two-hour break to go home for lunch. Cheque Restaurante would not be fully embraced in Spain until the country joined the European market.

In 1988 Sodexho entered the British food services market, which was dominated by a few major players, especially in the business & industry sector, so the group used the healthcare-focused approach that had been successful in the U.S. Sodexho signed its first contract with the Glasgow Royal Infirmary, Scotland's second-biggest hospital with a capacity of 900 patients. This contract became a springboard for the group's development in the U.K., where Sodexho soon won other new healthcare clients, first in London and then in Yorkshire. In 1992, the group was awarded a residential services contract with the St Mary's NHS Trust hospital's prestigious Lindo Wing, which has cared for members of the Royal Family.

As Sodexho's employees recall, the Glasgow Royal Infirmary's decision to hand over its residential and food services to this small French company surprised many people. It was Seiler's that played a decisive role in convincing the hospital's managers – who visited U.S. hospitals managed by the company – of the group's experience and skills. By positioning itself as a service provider with expertise in healthcare, the British subsidiary stood out from the competition and rapidly grew.

Sodexho strengthened its position in the meal voucher industry at home and abroad in the mid-1980s. In 1986, following its acquisition of French company Chèque-Restaurant, the group merged that business with Ticket-Repas under the Chèque-Restaurant brand. This allowed Sodexho, the second-ranked player worldwide, to place third in the French market, putting the pressure on market leader Ticket-Restaurant, an Accor group subsidiary whose communications efforts were plentiful and highly instructive.

Under the management of Albert George, the young team honed its marketing strategy and played up its innovative and creative talents to avoid being bulldozed by Ticket-Restaurant. The organization expanded by moving into Italy, Luxembourg and then Chile, where it leveraged its food services presence to develop its meal voucher operations. Very favorable market conditions and a partnership with Citibank led the business to break even within 18 months.

Faced with the dramatically weakening remote-site market, most significantly in the Middle East and Africa, Sodexho once again drew on the patience, determination and self-confidence that had helped the group overcome many difficult challenges. "We intend to maintain the strong positions we hold in all our markets. Faced with decreased margins, we will continue our efforts to reinforce our business in markets where we are a leader," declared Pierre Bellon, thus making it clear that Sodexho was determined to maintain its position as a global leader in remote sites.

IMPROVING THE QUALITY OF LIFE FOR PRISONERS

Sodexho's entry into the correctional services segment was motivated by two factors.

First, the group was convinced it could improve prisoners' quality of life and use reinsertion programs to facilitate their resettlement into the outside world, both socially and professionally. Were it not for this conviction, the group surely would not have taken on the challenge of entering this difficult and often misrepresented market.

The second element occurred in 1987 with the French government's program to design, build and furnish 25 new correctional facilities whose non-penal services would be outsourced to the private sector. Sodexho seized the opportunity to bid, and it won contracts for partial management of five facilities in the Paris region and elsewhere in France in 1989.

In February 1990, the group created a specialized subsidiary, SIGES, to better address the needs of the sector. From its first foray into correctional services, Sodexho would provide traditional residential and maintenance services and transportation as well as manage workshops, provide medical care and vocational training, and assist inmates in their job searches.

In the Middle East, remote-site opportunities had dried up, but the region's efforts at modernization over the past 15 years had created new opportunities for food services providers. Thanks to its experience in the region and familiarity with local cultures, Sodexho would soon enjoy success, signing contracts with the likes of the Universities of Jeddah (6,000 customers a day) and Riyadh (8,000 customers a day) in Saudi Arabia.

Meanwhile, at Sodexho's headquarters in France, an ambitious new project was about to see the light.

An Ill Wind…

It was a company tradition to use code names thought up by Pierre Bellon for major strategic initiatives to maintain confidentiality. He named his newest, top-secret initiative "Operation Dodo"[1]. It would require all of his energy and that of his most trusted colleagues for several months.

Operation Dodo marked a major, highly difficult episode in Sodexho's history, one that began with great hopes for the future and ended abruptly with another one of the financial world's unexpected reversals. Once again, the Operation Dodo episode involved certain elements and protagonists of the JBI affair, including the joint heads of Accor, Paul Dubrule and Gérard Pélisson.

Bellon had never made a secret of his ambitions for Sodexho's development. The founder's pioneering, conquering spirit had led the group to rank among the industry's global leaders in just 20 years. After its

1. "Dodo" is a word French children use to refer to going to bed, similar to "beddy-byes" in English. It also refers to the sleeping cars on a train, which were at one time a signature service of Wagons-Lits.

launch as a local operation, Sodexho had expanded to become a national and then an international organization, holding its own against such market behemoths as Aramark, Marriott Management Services and Gardner Merchant while maintaining its financial independence. Remarkable in many ways, family-owned Sodexho's growth and situation also presented new challenges. To embrace the future, the group would have to become much bigger, as Bellon realized in 1981 when Sodexho tried to join forces with JBI.

Clearly, the solution was to team up with another industry leader, preferably a European company whose strengths fit seamlessly with Sodexho's own. When the opportunity presented itself, the chance to form an alliance with Compagnie Internationale des Wagons-Lits et du Tourisme (CIWLT) was especially appealing because, at least at first, the potential partner seemed so willing.

Created in Belgium at the end of the 19th century, CIWLT had built its reputation on a network of dining and sleeping cars on trains traveling through Europe. Its crown jewel was the magical Orient Express, the height of luxury in rail travel and an object of fantasy for many a generation of romantics. By the late 1980s, however, the company's image had lost most of its sparkle following diversification into

Wagons-lits Says Sodexho Has Acquired 17.5% Stake

AP-DOW JONES NEWS SERVICE

BRUSSELS – Cie. Internationale des Wagons-Lits & du Tourisme SA said Sodexho has acquired 17.5% of the Belgian travel and tourism group.

The Wall Street Journal, January 13, 1989

Italianen treden in Kapitaal Wagons-Lits

Sodexho via dubbele overname grootste cateringggroep in België

De Financieel Ekonomische TIJD,
April 9, 1991

the tourism and hotel industries. It was also a long-standing player in the food services market via Eurest, created in 1970 through an equal partnership with Swiss company Nestlé – which sold off its stake in 1984 to focus on its core business.

"The Madonna of the sleeping cars," as the Orient Express was known among the press, had gone into a lull and was having trouble rousing itself, despite recent modernization efforts. It was clear that CIWLT was looking to restructure operations. In a climate of ongoing market consolidation, its main competitors made it clear at once that they were interested in acquiring portions of CIWLT's business.

Eurest was the most "European" of the French food services providers, among which it ranked third. It enjoyed an especially strong position in the Netherlands, Germany and Austria, markets where Sodexho had little presence. Thanks to Nestlé's involvement in its early days, the company had developed an approach based on nutritional research, technology and strategy that had enabled it to grow rapidly. In fact, Nestlé had greatly influenced Eurest's corporate culture. But ever since Nestlé's withdrawal, Eurest had become somewhat of an orphan within the group, where it was treated as an afterthought in investment decisions and project planning.

As interested as ever in developments in the food services sector, Pierre Bellon watched Eurest with a keen eye; he was fully aware that Sodexho's main strategic interests were at stake. If Sodexho's historical rival Générale de Restauration joined forces with Eurest, it would be a major setback for the group in its pursuit of the global leadership it had patiently embarked upon years before.

The more Bellon considered the idea of teaming up with Eurest, the more convinced he became that this was the right thing to do. As he had demonstrated in 1981, his main interest lay in food services. He planned a course of action to acquire CIWLT and then combine the group's travel agency business with that of Havas, American Express or Carlson Travel, in addition to divesting the group's hotel business. After a long series of negotiations, the possibility of an acquisition finally seemed likely at the end of 1988.

The agreement between the two companies was made public on January 12, 1989 in a joint press release announcing that Sodexho had acquired 17.5% of CIWLT's capital. Bellon explained his strategy behind the move to all of Sodexho's managers the following day:

Bod volkomen onvoldoende
Sodexho hekelt prijs Wagons-Lits en stapt naar Bankkommissie

TIJD, October 24, 1991

Il gruppo è leader europeo nella ristorazione collettiva

Ribadito da Sodexho l'impegno in Italia

ORE 12, November 7 , 1991

"I believe in the future of CIWLT… It was our belief that a major investment in this international services company would help us in the pursuit of our objectives. This is a goal I have already addressed, especially in considering the 1992 European horizon. Secondly, the complementary nature of our businesses and markets would allow each of us to strengthen our respective positions in the food services industry in Europe and the rest of the world… Eurest and Sodexho owe their growth to the hard work of their managers and teams, as well as the quality of services offered to clients and customers. There can be no doubt that bringing the two groups together offers us both the best prospects for future growth."

The event marked a milestone in Sodexho's history – or so it seemed – because it was the first time Sodexho had linked fates with another entity. Bellon was fully aware of the consequences the change would have for his employees and himself. "My first objective is for the merger to succeed. It won't be easy; we've seen other mergers of this size fail in the past," he stated in the press. "I was concerned about my own ability to participate in the management of a group I didn't create and share management responsibilities with someone else," he admits.

In late 1989, the alliance began to combine operations and merge its management organization, with some of Sodexho's employees relocating from Montigny-le-Bretonneux to Eurest's offices in Levallois-Perret, just west of Paris. Soon, however, new tensions emerged, perhaps not surprising given the two companies' strong, unique corporate cultures. While Eurest embraced traditional culinary arts, for example, Sodexho took a more businesslike approach, focusing on delivering results and gaining new market share. Clashes were inevitable.

But the heart of the problem lay elsewhere – in the three main partners' highly divergent views, which would eventually wipe out months of hard work. Behind the scenes, power plays and struggles for influence gained momentum as one of the partners began to insist that CIWLT's hotel business be sold to Accor. This again placed Sodexho on a collision course with its old adversary.

The JBI affair was still in everyone's memory, of course, and many wondered if history was about to repeat itself – not quite, but Accor seemed to be using the same playbook, skillfully maneuvering people into changing loyalties and getting a shareholder to withdraw, making Bellon and Sodexho's position untenable.

Challenge to bid for Wagons-Lits

DISGRUNTLED Wagons-Lits shareholders are challenging Accor's FFr2.2bn ($390m) bid to take over the Franco-Belgian travel company in the Brussels commercial court, throwing the plan into a state of acrimony and confusion.

Financial Times, November 14, 1991

The breaking point finally came when Accor acquired a stake in CIWLT and Paul Dubrule and Gérard Pélisson gained seats on CIWLT's Board. In response, Bellon held a press conference on October 2, 1990 to discuss the consequences of the new balance of power. Sodexho was no longer CIWLT's preferred business partner, he noted, and the hotel operations would most likely be managed by Accor. Moreover, there were doubts about the future of the Eurest–Sodexho alliance, despite its potential for achieving global leadership in the contract food services industry.

Bellon could have fought back, but he realized that conflict with the other CIWLT shareholders would have been detrimental to the company's customers, its employees and the shareholders themselves. He was also aware that the other shareholders were unlikely to reach an agreement and that a three-headed management team at Wagons-Lits would severely crimp his room to maneuver. Convinced of Sodexho's promising future, Bellon therefore chose to withdraw, regaining his freedom and Sodexho's total independence.

The financial aspects of the alliance's unwinding took another five years, with each episode serialized in the business press. As soon as Sodexho officially announced its withdrawal, Accor made a public offer for CIWLT, valuing shares at 218.10 euros despite having recently paid 315.17 euros for its initial stake. For Sodexho and the other CIWLT minority shareholders belonging to Deminor, a European investor rights organization, this was clearly unacceptable. They immediately brought legal proceedings against Accor in the Brussels commercial court, which ruled that Accor would have to pay a higher price. The Brussels court of appeals upheld the ruling, as did Belgium's court of cassation, the country's court of final resort. CIWLT's minority shareholders, including Sodexho, eventually received 315.17 euros per share.

The cash proceeds were soon reinvested in Sodexho's international expansion, providing a silver lining for the whole affair. As Bellon succinctly put it, "The alliance with Wagons-Lits was a strategic failure but a financial success."

Together

Pierre Bellon was greatly affected by his inability to carry out a strategic move he deemed valuable for Sodexho, according to family members, friends and employees. "But, once again, he proved he knew that what's important is not how many times you get

Paul Bonnette

knocked down but how many times you get back up," reflects Paul Bonnette, executive vice president of human resources at the time.

As it turned out, it was far from the end of the world for Sodexho. The difficult challenge of integrating the two companies would have consumed too much of Sodexho's resources and energy, slowing down its international development. Additionally, had things turned out differently, what role would the new shareholder have played in the group's management?

Long aware of the importance of people, Bellon soon intensified his efforts to re-energize Sodexho teams in the wake of what he saw as a failure. He soon discovered, however, that employees did not see things in the same light. In fact, the values on which he had built Sodexho were as strong as ever.

Convinced that the CIWLT affair had slowed down the group's expansion, in October 1990 Bellon initiated an in-depth process to rethink Sodexho's strategic vision and corporate mission.

With the help of Michel Dubois, group senior vice president, Planning, Innovation and Quality, a questionnaire was developed and distributed to the group's 100 top executives. Michel Dubois received 70 responses, in which respondents shared their thoughts, perceptions and suggestions on six themes:

- Identifying the cultural heritage and values on which the group's identity was based.
- Outlining a long-term vision and objectives for the group, and identifying the challenges it faced.
- Finding, predicting and anticipating constraints imposed by the environment.
- Identifying the group's strengths and weaknesses.
- Evaluating the group's management of its subsidiaries.
- Studying possible changes in its capital structure.

In January and February 1991, 50 department and subsidiary heads – excluding top group management – were divided up into workgroups that examined the six themes. The results of their work were presented to the Executive Committee on April 3, 1991.

There was no doubt about it. Far from feeling discouraged, the group's managers reaffirmed their confidence in the group and their belief in its mission and values. And they continued to support its goal of "becoming the world's number-one provider of outsourced food services" and the accelerated international development needed to reach this goal.

Last but not least, the managers expressed their desire that Sodexho remain family-owned – in other words, independent – "And 99% of them agreed on this point," recalls Bernard Carton.

"The group's ambition is the sum of the ambitions of its managers."

During the discussions, Bellon reaffirmed that financial independence was part of the company's strategic bedrock, the foundation for its growth. "Maintaining financial control is not a goal in itself; what we need is for our shareholders to invest in the group's long-term development rather than desert us the moment the prospect of immediate capital gains appears on the horizon. Our shareholders are responsible for appointing the group's leaders based on their skills, and they participate in developing our strategic orientation. As long as the group performs well and improves its results, a stable group of shareholders is unlikely to change our management or strategy. Loyal shareholders demonstrate confidence in the managers of their group and work to protect the group from outside forces, financial raiders and the competition."

Driven by its goal to become "*the* benchmark in all areas of our business," Sodexho identified areas for progress: client focus, human resources, reactivity of the organization to new market conditions, communication skills and financial results.

Optimistic and confident that the group had what it needed to pursue growth, Sodexho's employees looked to the future. The second Sodexho World Innovation Forum, held in Lille in northern France in June 1991, testified to this enthusiasm. The forum

Fifth Sodexho World Innovation Forum,
Paris, 1998

introduced the group's 500 participating employees, as well as nearly 80 clients, suppliers and journalists, to 38 innovations developed by its employees around the globe.

Thanks to the efforts of the innovation department, created in 1988, Sodexho was able to efficiently and methodically organize the bottom-up collection of information about innovations developed in its 35 host countries. In 1991, the Conviv'styles system – which entailed carrying out onsite lifestyle studies for business & industry clients – was awarded first prize at the forum, as well as special recognition from the audience.

A few days earlier, 450 companies and over 7,000 athletes had participated in the fourth World Corporate Games, also held in Lille. Sodexho was the event's main sponsor, providing food services for athletes, journalists and VIPs at the event while also participating in the competition. For the first time in the group's history, employees from North and South America, Europe, Africa and Asia gathered to uphold the company's honor. The efforts of the group's 350 participating athletes did not go unrewarded: they won 30 medals and, thanks to the ten nationalities represented, Sodexho received recognition for fielding the most international team.

The Sodexho Laundry Services pavilion at the 2002 Innovation Forum in Chicago, Illinois (U.S.)

CONVIV'STYLES: A MAJOR INNOVATION

The same spirit that led the group to segment its markets according to clients in 1984 led it to create an exclusive new tool in 1990 that offered an unprecedented level of customer-oriented analysis.

Developed by the group's business & industry subsidiary in France, the Conviv'styles tool, unique in the market, allowed the company to analyze customers by taking into account the special features of each site and to zero in on differing customer expectations. The system was aimed at helping Sodexho personalize its products and services according to the specific customers at each site.

Inspired by the socio-lifestyles method, which categorizes consumers according to distinctive lifestyle groups, Conviv'styles identified six main customer families, each of which corresponded to a separate consumer segment with unique expectations: Dreamers, Habit-formers, Traditionalists, Achievers, Easy-goers and Perfectionists.

Customer analysis was used to create a detailed profile of those employees who partook of food services provided onsite and those who did not. Menus were then developed based on the customer-site profile. Ultimately, the program allowed Sodexho to create the most attractive offering possible for customers at a given site.

Over the years, the Conviv'styles model would be adapted to the group's other markets and regions, resulting in Restau'styles, Conviv'styles Juniors, Italy's Archipelago program, and Customer Profiling in the U.K. Most recently, the group drew upon the Conviv'styles method in creating the global PERSONIX program. This exclusive new marketing tool, developed under the leadership of Laurent Cousin, group senior vice president, Food Offering, Research and Development, allows Sodexho to analyze and describe consumer behavior in the workplace.

Laurent Cousin

Pierre Bellon was deeply moved as he saluted the efforts of Sodexho's employees before a full stadium. The group's athletes had shown that they were fighting for a united cause: Sodexho.

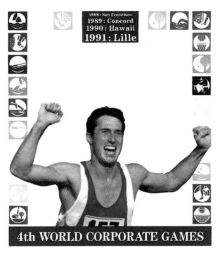

The Fourth World Corporate Games, 1991

10

In Full Sail

Following its failed attempts to team up with Eurest, Sodexho concentrated its efforts on international development via organic growth, acquisitions and partnerships. Within three years, it would launch operations in 25 new countries. It was also an important moment for the group's corporate identity, which began to take shape thanks to initiatives in corporate communications and human resources. Sodexho was committed to communicating policies and innovations from one subsidiary to the next, wherever they originated. The group also worked on expanding its recently renamed "service voucher" operations into new regions and areas of service.

Faced with an economic crisis and the Gulf War in the first half of the 1990s, Sodexho demonstrated the same doggedness that had helped it through many a rough patch in the past: the group was determined not to cede a square inch of its territory to the competition. But the unexpected alliance of Générale de

Restauration and Orly Restauration in 1993, which allowed the companies to gain a leadership position in France[1], would once again raise the question – more pointedly than ever – of the possibility of an alliance for Sodexho.

The Sun Rises in the East

In 1989, the same year that Sodexho signed its agreement with CIWLT, a seemingly impossible event changed the course of world history. On November 9, 1989, before cameras from around the world, young people from East and West Germany tore down the Berlin Wall, the symbol of the Cold War that had divided Berlin since 1961.

It was the end of an era and the demise of Communism in Eastern Europe. In the wake of political liberalization pursued by Mikhail Gorbachev starting in 1986, the entire Communist bloc would undergo profound change. More than his *Perestroika* program, introduced to the world in a book published simultaneously in English and Russian in 1987, it would be Gorbachev's policy of *glasnost* ("openness") that would accelerate the demise of the Soviet regime. Throughout the vast Soviet Union, people took

1. Sodexho regained the top-ranked position in the French market in 1998.

advantage of liberalized policies to speak freely against the regime, reviving the underground nationalist movement.

One after another, the Soviet Republics began to declare their independence. In 1989, the first free elections in Eastern Europe since 1948 were held in Poland, and Vaclav Havel was elected President of the Czech Republic. Democracy was spreading through Eastern Europe like wildfire.

Sodexho was not a company to sit on the sidelines during this period of upheaval. The group began to carefully launch operations in Eastern Europe, not only in food services, but also in service vouchers and remote sites.

Although as early as 1988 Pierre Bellon had made the Soviet Union "a development project for Sodexho," the group chose to proceed cautiously, given the region's upheaval and uncertain future. The company's development in the region did not pick up speed until Bellon's 1991 visit to Moscow with the CNPF Association.

Sodexho signed its first remote-site contract in the region in 1992. The following year, to prepare its launch in a country that was slowly beginning to embrace the notion of a market economy, Rémi Baudin headed to Moscow. Within a few months,

SODEXHO IN THE USSR, ACCORDING TO MICHEL DUBOIS

"After attending a presentation of Mikhail Gorbachev's book, *Perestroika,* in 1987, I sent Pierre Bellon a short memo: 'New opportunities for Sodexho in the USSR?'

"The following year, after discussing it with the Executive Committee, Bellon decided to make the USSR a target for expansion, and he asked me to lead the project.

"I headed to Moscow in July 1988 with a Russian-speaking colleague and an architect. Upon our arrival, we quickly realized that, more than food services, the country's companies and institutions were in dire need of modern kitchens and equipment! We decided to organize a large exhibition of kitchen equipment in Leningrad (today St. Petersburg)

with the support of the city's mayor. Upon our return to France, we told French manufacturers about the exhibition, which took place in February-March 1989 and was a great success.

"That first experience in the Soviet Union allowed us to make numerous contacts and served as a launching pad for the development of Sodexho's core businesses in Russia. The fall of the Berlin Wall in November 1989 only accelerated our growth. Despite a chaotic political situation, we managed to maintain and widen our circle of contacts, which would lead to the signing of our first remote-site contract in 1992."

after remodeling the kitchen of an engineering school to house the group's central kitchen facilities, Sodexho began signing its first contracts with Western companies that had opened offices in Moscow.

In 1992, Sodexho made its first foray into two other markets of the former Communist bloc. In Hungary, the group acquired the second-ranked player, with sales of 8.7 million euros and 600 employees. In the Czech Republic, Sodexho took a very different approach, building its local business from scratch. In both countries, Sodexho sought to concurrently develop its food services and service voucher businesses, as it would do whenever possible in all new markets from then on.

That same year, Sodexho became a majority shareholder in the Finnish company Polarkesti. Created in 1979 by the hotel and restaurant group Arctia, the "Little North Star" had propelled itself into the third-ranked position in only a decade. Kirsti Piponius, who was responsible for the company's success, would manage the subsidiary until 2003. "When we launched Polarkesti, our resources were very limited," she recalls. "I slowly started recruiting a team, outlining purchasing procedures and building an offering. At that time, not only was the outsourced catering services industry in its infancy, with barely 10% market penetration, but it also did not enjoy a positive reputation. This actually ended up working in our favor. As trailblazers in the industry, we were quickly able to develop standards that suited us and our way of getting

Polarkesti was acquired on December 17, 1992. *Seated:* Rémi Baudin *(second from left)* and Kirsti Piponius *(right)*

Kirsti Piponius

Sodexho-België gaat met overnemingen Belgorest en Restaura naar 4 mld. omzet

DE STANDAARD, April 9, 1991.

things done. From the very beginning, for example, we created a client and customer satisfaction survey. We also implemented a bonus system to make sure that our employees knew their efforts were recognized and that they felt pride in the job they were doing. Our reputation as an innovative company grew over the years, which is surely what made us attractive to Sodexho!" True to its innovative heritage, the Finnish company would be the driving force behind the group's first National Innovation Forum in Finland in 1996.

The group's entry into the Turkish market occurred in 1992, when it launched food services and service vouchers at the same time, followed in 1994 by the launch of Sodexho's operations in Poland.

While enjoying success in its newest markets, Sodexho was not about to neglect the countries where it had already established a presence. The group had indeed come a long way; after its first attempt to enter the Belgian market nearly a quarter of a century earlier, which also marked its first venture outside France, it had become a top player in Belgium's food services market after acquiring Belgorest and Restaura in 1991. Over the years, the group had enjoyed a number of successes in Belgium, where it had become the top issuer of service vouchers. It was also in Belgium that the group's voucher production unit received ISO 9002 certification, making Sodexho the first service voucher company worldwide to be so certified.

Also the leading issuer of service vouchers in Germany, the group would renew its efforts in the local food services market nearly 15 years after failing in its first attempts to enter the market. In 1991, the group acquired Eiring, which would remain under the leadership of its founder, Harry Eiring.

During the first half of the 1990s, Sodexho expanded its service voucher and card activities in Latin America. There and around the world, Albert George and his team were driven to catch up to the world's leading service voucher issuer, Accor, as quickly as possible. The group became the top player in Mexico upon its acquisition of Prestamex, and it also created a subsidiary in 1991 in Venezuela, where the childcare voucher system was conceived and the young local team managed to sign agreements with 600 childcare facilities within only a few months. In 1994, Sodexho entered Colombia's food services and service voucher markets within a two-month period; to increase their chances of success in a market full of opportunity, the two subsidiaries decided to work in

Philippe Voraz

tandem. Thanks to the creative energy of its teams, Sodexho rapidly became the leader in that country's service voucher industry.

Operations in South America, which was one of Sodexho's first growth regions, proved their potential under the leadership of Philippe Voraz. Like Michel Landel, Voraz belonged to the generation of young managers who had been trained in Africa and who were dedicated to bringing the group's philosophy to life throughout their careers. "I immediately felt passionate about Sodexho," admits Voraz. "I felt inspired by the group's honesty, its respect for people and the work ethic it embraced. From the very beginning, I was lucky enough to work with men like Yves Bayon and Michel Landel, who personified these values."

In 1988, when Voraz took on the responsibility of the group's South American subsidiary, its 2,000 employees provided food and management services in two countries, Brazil and Chile. The early 1990s marked the start of a new phase of development, with Sodexho entering five new countries in the region within 15 years. Beginning with Argentina, where the group renewed its efforts in 1991 with a small remote-site setup in Patagonia, it went on to enter the Venezuelan market in 1993, followed by Colombia in

1994 and Peru in 1999, finally completing its South American network with the 2001 launch of operations in Costa Rica.

Given an unstable political and economic context, Sodexho chose to base its expansion on partnerships with recognized local players. But the most crucial element in the group's expansion was Voraz's pursuit of talented individuals and entrepreneurs at the local level. "Sodexho owes its local growth to the South Americans who built the business," underscores Claudia Guiloff, responsible for human resources in the region. Thanks to the group's policy of local recruitment and training, employees were faced with a wealth of opportunities for personal and professional development. Group policies on local hiring and training and internal promotion continue to play a major role in the development of human resources. Today, all of the group's subsidiaries in the region are headed by managers hired locally. Diversity has also played a major role, with four women sitting on the 11-member regional Executive Commitee.

Furthermore, the group's dedication to facilitating mobility between subsidiaries at the managerial level contributed to the sharing of expertise and career development.

Pierre Bellon and Patrice Douce
with employees in front of the Chilean
subsidiary's headquarters

JUNAEB: MAKING EDUCATION UNIVERSALLY ACCESSIBLE

Since 1998, Sodexho has participated in the Chilean government's JUNAEB program to help make public schools accessible to all children.

Located in poor outlying regions as well as in city centers, these schools provide an education to underprivileged children, some of whom travel great distances on foot to attend.

In many cases, the primary reason that families send their children to school is so that they can have something to eat.

Sodexho's Chilean subsidiary developed a special food offering for the program (including breakfast and lunch), adapted to the children's nutritional needs and the widespread network of schools. Since getting involved in the program, Sodexho has provided meals to 220,000 Chilean schoolchildren daily.

Dedicated to participating in training and hiring programs in all the South American markets where it has a presence, Sodexho continues to enrich the talent pool for future generations of managers and has been recognized for its positive influence as an employer in the region.

"We Make a World of Difference"

The Sodexho Management Institute (SMI) opened its doors in 1992 as one of the first management training centers to be created by a French company and the culmination of years of effort by Pierre Bellon.

Developed in partnership with Lyons' International School of Management, the center's program was targeted toward the group's top 200 managers. Based largely on an exchange of experience, the program included an outline, provided by Bellon, of the group's history, philosophy and values from its earliest days.

"The SMI's role has always been to open the minds of our managers to change and the group's international context, while also continually helping them make progress," says Elisabeth Carpentier, group executive vice president, Human Resources. "Over the years, we adapted the concept and content of training to the group's evolving needs as we continued to grow and enter new markets. The programs we developed at the SMI continue to play a central role in allowing the group to extend a common culture, build a shared vision of management, and capitalize on expertise developed in each of our markets and activities. Because we are in the client services business,

"Managers also need to be trained."

Elisabeth Carpentier

The Sodexho Management Institute (SMI) trains managers from around the globe

it is up to our men and women to make a difference; they are the heart of our competitive advantage. It is therefore our duty to provide the tools they need to evolve and adapt their skills to the changing needs of the world market."

The SMI was only one incarnation of Bellon's conviction that, "Managers also need to be trained, because honing their skills can help make a company more competitive." He liked to remind his colleagues, "We are all equally inexpert, because every day we're faced with a new situation."

Pierre Bellon benefited from a particularly clear vision of what was at stake thanks to his participation in the Young Managers Association (CJD) starting in the late 1950s as a young employee in the family business.

Bellon's personal convictions would shape many initiatives, both within and outside of the group, as exemplified by the creation of the Management Progress Association within the CNPF in 1986. The association — which caused quite a stir within the CNPF — was intended, according to Bellon, not to teach managers how to run their companies but rather to help them reflect upon and exchange their ideas about the management and corporate methods that could help them adapt their companies to evolving market conditions; 20 years on, the association has grown to 203 local chapters and more than 3,800 members.

Bellon would also demonstrate a passion for the writings of leading figures in strategy and management, including Peter Drucker, Kenichi Ohmae, Tom Peters and Robert Waterman. Rather than keeping what he learned to himself, he never missed an opportunity to share it with his most trusted colleagues. "Pierre Bellon always followed a certain guiding principle: he understood that leaders of rapidly growing companies are continually faced with the challenge of never having run a business that size," points out Albert George, former group chief operating officer, Sodexho Alliance. "Therefore, he believed it was essential to draw upon external resources where management was concerned." Many articles and excerpts would be circulated among the group's leaders before being discussed during one of its regularly held management seminars.

But theories and models were meant to serve as building blocks, not objectives, and were challenged every time they ran into market reality. "Do it, undo it and do it again," Bellon would often say.

STARTING FROM THE HEART OF THE MATTER:
SODEXHO AND THE SOCIAL SCIENCES

As he has demonstrated time and time again, Pierre Bellon is passionate about the role companies play in society.

Not only did he dedicate a significant amount of his time and energy to the question, but he also made sure that Sodexho maintained ongoing partnerships with researchers in the social sciences. Beyond satisfying his never-ending curiosity about the matter, Bellon sought to better understand the men and women he employed as well as the ties binding them to the group.

In 1983, the group opened its doors to an ethnologist eager to learn more about Sodexho's "tribe." This first ethnological experience, which focused on the group's dining facilities, led to the development of a unique methodology of action plans related to service quality that engaged those employees involved in the service offering in quality control processes that took place before services were delivered.

In the years that followed, other projects were undertaken with sociologists, philosophers and organizational researchers, and a research department was created. The wide-ranging research included topics that dealt with understanding the organic growth process, the cultural and organizational drivers of innovation and the ways in which employees embrace organizational change. In each case, the projects reflected the company's position on the development timeline and were designed in response to clearly defined needs.

For the most part based on active participation, this research proved a highly valuable tool for Sodexho, as it allowed the company to reflect upon its role and consider its initiatives in a wider context.

In the early 1990s, as it would on many other occasions, Sodexho again demonstrated its ability to adapt and its managers' determination never to be limited by outlines or organizational models. "Organizational structures," notes Bellon, "are meant to help our women and men do business." In September 1993, a trade magazine published an article – "Sodexho's Soft Revolution" – on the evolution of the group's organizational structure.

Ten years after implementing a segmented approach and creating its business & industry, healthcare and education subsidiaries, the group had decided to create a division for France. Under the responsibility of Jean-Michel Dhenain, it would oversee the entire range of services provided by the group in the French market.

"It is not so much a question of restructuring the group; it is more about simply adapting to the evolution and growth of our activities," Dhenain stated at the time. "We found that we could more efficiently manage our clients and teams under a single management structure." The group also started to consider the possibility of benefiting from horizontal synergies within the same field of activity on an international level; this would lead to the birth of "world market champions" three years later.

We make a world of difference

The group adopts a new visual identity, including the "We make a world of difference" tagline in 1993

September 1993 marked the renewal of Sodexho's brand image to leverage its increasing diversity. The group updated its original three-teacup logo by adding a spectrum of blues and the new slogan, "We make a world of difference." It would also utilize a border of images depicting an increasingly wide range of services in certain documents. That same year, Sodexho received the prize for best financial communications from French communications magazine *Stratégies* for its shareholder and financial publications, unified under the group's new visual identity.

Under the Sodexho Pass brand, the group's service voucher and card business also sought to bring together the range of names it used in different markets. The creation of Sodexho Pass International in 1995 helped to unite the operation around the globe.

"Of course, our communications efforts evolved over the years," recalls Clodine Pincemin, group executive vice president, Communications and Sustainable Development, "but we were always guided by two fundamental aspects of our business. It is impossible to understand the group's communications without keeping in mind that the thousands of employees working onsite around the globe – representing 97% of our workforce – play the biggest role in conveying our image to clients and that our lines of business were, for a long time, little-known. Therefore, our communications efforts were based on two strategic goals: strengthening the pride and feeling of belonging among our employees, and building the group's reputation and image while continuously adapting to the evolution of the group."

In this area as in various others, the group would learn many a valuable lesson as it evolved and grew increasingly aware of the important role played by communications in its development.

The group's 1983 listing on the Paris Stock Exchange marked a milestone in its history. As it became better known, it had to learn new communications skills, especially in the area of investor relations. However, the role of communications would really start to take shape with the creation of a corporate communications department in 1991, headed by Pincemin, who until then had overseen communications efforts in France and Europe.

While internal communications remained a priority, the group also began to sponsor international sporting events. "A 1991 survey of our employees revealed that they did not feel closely tied to the Sodexho brand. To remedy this situation, we began signing our first sponsorships of such major sporting events as the Tour de France, which was able to offer

A selection of images depicting an increasingly diverse range of services

"WELCOME, MISTER JOHN"

For the first time in Sodexho's history, an institutional film was developed in 1987, the brainchild of Clodine Pincemin, head of external communications at the time. Shot on the group's sites in France, Italy, the U.S., Canada, Oman and Saudi Arabia, "Welcome, Mister John" presented all of the group's activities across the globe.

"We had to fight for the financial resources we needed to accomplish the project," recalls Pincemin. "At the time, there wasn't the recognized need for corporate communications that there is today, but the work and energy we invested in the project certainly paid off."

In 1988, "Welcome, Mister John" received first prize in the consumer business and services category at the International Festival of Audiovisual Programs in Biarritz. It was only the first in a long series of awards the group would win for its internal, financial and corporate communications efforts.

An excerpt from Sodexho's 1987 institutional film, *"Welcome, Mister John"*

Official partner of the Tour de France

World Youth Day (WYD),
Paris, 1997

"Strengthening the pride and feeling of belonging among our employees and building the group's reputation and image."

participants and guests a satisfying meal for the first time, thanks to our teams," explains Pincemin. "At the same time, we also increased our sales efforts toward major international sporting events, while maintaining a high level of selectivity so that our employees could feel proud of what we were doing.

"These efforts strengthened the group's image as it became better known, both outside the company and within. It was a very important motivating factor."

In 1992 Sodexho provided food services to the Albertville Winter Olympics in France and the Barcelona Summer Olympics in Spain, as well as the IAAF World Championships in Athletics in Stuttgart, Germany. As the years passed, the group leveraged its international network and unsurpassed skills to become a leading partner of major events bringing together thousands of people from around the globe, including the Olympics, the Rugby World Cup and World Youth Day (WYD). It gradually phased out its sponsorship of athletic events as it began to focus its resources on the fight against hunger and malnutrition. Sodexho felt it had a role to play in this struggle, which would also add an emotional dimension to the brand and contribute to its employees' pride and feeling of belonging.

REACHING FOR THE STARS

1993: Creation of the School for Chefs.

Always ready to team up with the most unexpected partners, Sodexho joined forces with one of French gastronomy's shining stars, Marc Veyrat. This outstanding chef is well known for his ability to coax the most daring

France's top chefs with Bruno But, director of the School for Chefs

flavors from plants he harvests himself in the mountains. An ardent supporter of the quality of food in everyday life, he likes to remind people that "Fine dining begins with what we eat every day."

The School for Chefs reflects Sodexho's desire to provide its chefs with the highest levels of gastronomic training. Sessions take place in Veyrat's restaurant, *l'Auberge de l'Eridan*, on the shores of Lake Annecy in the French Alps, where Sodexho's chefs have a chance to make innovative methods their own, unleash their creative forces and refresh their menus.

The partnership grew to include five other leading French chefs[1] – whose role is to select the best ingredients, share their expertise in the preparation of meals and contribute to the development of healthy, balanced dishes – in order to improve the daily offerings in Sodexho's food services facilities.

1. Photo: Jean-Michel Lorain (*La Côte Saint-Jacques*, Joigny, www.cotesaintjacques.com), Michel Bras (Laguiole, www.michel-bras.com), Pierre Gagnaire (Paris 8th arrondissement, www.pierre-gagnaire.com), Olivier Roellinger (*Maison de Bricourt*, Cancale, www.maisons-de-bricourt.com), Jacques Chibois (*La Bastide Saint-Antoine*, Grasse, www.jacques-chibois.com), and Marc Veyrat (www.marcveyrat.fr).

SODEXHO'S PARTNERSHIPS WITH MAJOR EVENTS: A FEW MILESTONES

1988: Calgary Winter Olympics

1992: Albertville Winter and Special Olympics, France

1992: Barcelona Summer and Special Olympics, Spain

1993: IAAF World Championships in Athletics, Stuttgart, Germany

1993: Mediterranean Games, Cap d'Agde, France

1997: World Youth Day, Paris, France

1997: World Rowing Championships, Annecy, France

2000: Sydney Summer Olympics, Australia

2000: World Youth Day, Rome, Italy

2002: Commonwealth Games, Manchester, U.K.

2003: World Rugby Cup, Sydney, Australia

2005: IAAF World Championships in Athletics, Finland

2005: World Youth Day, Cologne, Germany

At the end of 1994, Pierre Bellon announced before the financial and economic press that the group was doing quite well. Reporters came away from the presentation remarking on the group's success and taking note of Bellon's comment, "I am convinced that we will soon witness changes in ownership among some of the world's top ten food and management services companies. Should opportunities of this nature arise, Sodexho will be ready to seize them. We have what it takes." Sodexho, they said, "is still hungry."

Third Era: 1984–1994

MAIN THEMES

Client focused

*

Entrepreneurs are allowed
to make mistakes

*

Financial independence

*

Consolidating the group's
achievements

FIGURES

During this period, Sodexho's revenues grew by a factor of three, from 563 million to 1.7 billion euros, at an average annual growth rate of 12%. Net income increased by a factor of five, from 18 to 97 million euros (including a 73 million euro capital gain on the sale of CIWLT), at an average annual growth rate of 18%.

Fourth Era (1995–2005)

CITIZEN OF THE WORLD

"My dream is not so much that Sodexho is number one as that it endures."

To complement its organic growth, in 1995, Sodexho adopted a strategy of external growth that would allow the group to attain and reinforce a position of global leadership, outpace its competitors in the American market and multiply its revenues by a factor of four within three years.

Now more than 300,000 strong, Sodexho's employees would face – and overcome – new challenges brought on by globalization.

As the group approached its 40th anniversary and Pierre Bellon prepared to step down as CEO, he set in motion a new corporate mission project that would open a fresh chapter in Sodexho's history.

11

The Alliance or the Need for Acquisitions

"The Executive Committee resisted the idea, so Pierre Bellon went along with them." Patrice Douce, then president, was referring to the group's decision in 1992 not to pursue the acquisition of Gardner Merchant, the top-ranked food services company in continental Europe, the U.K. and Ireland. The latter had been put up for sale by its parent company, the U.K. group Trusthouse Forte, as a way to focus on its core hotel business.

It seemed like an ideal opportunity to Bellon. An alliance with Gardner Merchant would allow Sodexho, recently recovered from its failed attempts to join forces with the Compagnie Internationale des Wagons-Lits, to strengthen its global position and

Leading Food and Management Services
Providers in the U.K. and Ireland
by Market Share in the Early 1990s

	Rank	Market Share
Gardner Merchant (Forte group)	1	34%
Sutcliff	2	24%
Compass	3	19%
ARA Services[1]	4	7%
Sodexho Services (U.K.)		< 1%

1. ARA Services would become Aramark in 1994.

gain an instant foothold in the U.K. market, where, despite success in the healthcare segment, it continued to trail the competition.

But the deal was not meant to be, at least for the time being. "We turned down the opportunity," recalls Douce, "because Gardner Merchant's management team was simply not interested in being acquired." At the end of the day, the company was purchased by its management with the support of U.K. investment fund CIN-Ven and the Forte group retained 25% of its capital.

By 1994, however, the situation had changed. The efforts of Gardner Merchant's shareholding managers had paid off and the company, now once again profitable and growing, was considering going public on the London Stock Exchange. Thanks to the close ties they had maintained with Gardner Merchant's managers, Bellon and his team were able to step in, convincing them that joining forces with Sodexho would be the surest way to safeguard the growth and longevity of the company.

Upon concluding what some would consider its most important strategic alliance, Sodexho became the world leader in the food services industry, a position it would have to fight tooth and nail to maintain. The global consolidation of the food services market was just beginning…

The World Leader

Pierre Bellon could not pass up such an opportunity to strengthen Sodexho's position in the U.K. and Ireland. "It was either the British, the Americans or us" is how he sums up the situation in 1994. "We pushed ahead because if we hadn't, we would have forever played a bit part in the U.K. market." But while the alliance with Gardner Merchant helped to complete Sodexho's coverage of the global marketplace, an entirely different process was at work in the negotiations that led to the U.K. company's acquisition on January 21, 1995.

This time, a public bid or hostile raid was out of the question. Having learned a valuable lesson from its unsuccessful attempt to join forces with the Compagnie Internationale des Wagons-Lits, the group was determined never again to ally itself with a company without the support of its management team.

Sodexho's annual report, fiscal year 1995

Hans Rijnierse

As it happened, Gardner Merchant and Sodexho discovered that they were kindred spirits despite distinctly different cultures, histories and nationalities. A spirit of teamwork and cooperation drove the alliance, which was finalized on January 21, 1995. "We were the ones who chose Sodexho, rather than the other way around," recalls Hans Rijnierse, managing director, Netherlands Food and Management Services, at the time a senior manager at Gardner Merchant and one of the driving forces behind the management buy-out.

Sodexho and Gardner Merchant also shared some important values, including a client-focused approach, an ongoing commitment to employees and ambitious growth objectives. "The two groups have been able to develop their activities at the national and international level as they share a common approach to responding to client needs, developing their teams and adhering to ambitious quality standards," read the press release announcing the acquisition. "This alliance is fully endorsed by Gardner Merchant's Board of Directors and its entire management team. The two companies share common values and one vision: to become *the* international benchmark in the food services industry."

The coming together of the two companies marked a major milestone for Sodexho, according to Bellon, and the beginning of a long commitment to the concept of alliances that would prevail in all future acquisitions. Two years later, the group's name and logo would be modified to reflect this spirit.

At a press conference on January 24, 1995, Bellon outlined the conditions of the alliance as agreed upon with Gardner Merchant's management team. "Gardner Merchant will maintain its autonomy and identity as an independent division with the same status as Sodexho's other subsidiaries. The current management team will remain in place, with its current level of responsibility. Managing director Gary Hawkes will become chairman and CEO of the company; furthermore, he will be appointed to the Sodexho Board of Directors and named vice president. Our collaboration will be based on the overriding principle that our two companies will maintain their own identities, autonomy and brands in every country where they have a presence."

Gardner Merchant brought with it 55,000 employees, revenues of 1.6 billion euros, a leadership position in the U.K., Ireland and the Netherlands, and a presence in ten other markets, helping make the alliance the world's biggest food services company. Having doubled

Sodexho's Revenues by Region

	Before Gardner Merchant fiscal year 1994	After Gardner Merchant fiscal year 1995
United Kingdom and Ireland	–	23%
France	39%	24%
Other European Countries	29%	25%
North America	19%	18%
Latin America	6%	4%
Rest of the World	7%	6%

GARDNER MERCHANT

Logo, 1995

Van Hecke, Gardner Merchant's
Dutch subsidiary

in size, Sodexho now counted 110,000 employees among its ranks and revenues of 3.3 billion euros. The analysts and financial markets that had until very recently criticized Sodexho's waiting game greeted the news with enthusiasm, and the group's share price quadrupled in only four months.

Strategically sound on many levels, the alliance allowed Sodexho to gain a foothold in the Netherlands and strengthen its leadership position in the global remote-site market through Gardner's specialized subsidiary, Kelvin.

Gardner Merchant's employees, reassured by the fact that the company's management team would be kept in place, saw the acquisition as a means of guaranteeing the longevity and growth of their company and putting an end to two years of uncertainty about its future. "I explained to my teams that we were safeguarding our future," explained Hans Rijnierse, then managing director of Gardner Merchant's Dutch subsidiary, Van Hecke. "Of course, it didn't happen overnight. It took some time for everyone to get used to the idea, especially given the cultural divide. After more than 20 years of belonging to a U.K. group whose corporate culture resembled our own, we suddenly found ourselves part of a family-controlled French group that was listed on the stock market!

"Looking back, I know Sodexho and Gardner Merchant made the right decision. We were able to carry out our vision and achieve, if not surpass, the objectives outlined at the beginning of the alliance. Our success was largely due to outstanding local leaders heading each subsidiary who embraced an entrepreneurial approach to managing activities at the local level."

In the U.S., Michel Landel, placed at the helm by Bellon, worked in tandem with Richard Hutchinson, former CEO of Gardner Merchant USA, to bring the two entities together. The task was not an easy one. The two men were responsible for merging three, rather than two, companies, since Gardner Merchant had acquired Morrison's Hospitality in the southeastern U.S. only a few months before joining forces with Sodexho.

Nevertheless, it would take less than a year for them to carry out their mission, while respecting their goals of retaining the combined groups' clients and employees and strengthening business development. Success was made possible through close collaboration between Landel and Hutchinson. Both were deeply dedicated to the new company's long-term prosperity. Based on their shared, aligned strategic vision for the medium and long term, representatives

Richard Hutchinson

from both companies formed working groups to identify new methods and potential synergies in the combined organization. These groups were also the source of the decision to change the companies' names so as to move forward under the unified Sodexho banner.

With a presence in 42 states, Sodexho's American subsidiary, which had doubled in size and now ranked fourth in the American market, was poised to pursue major growth opportunities. However, Bellon and the company's senior managers knew that Sodexho was not yet where it needed to be to compete with the likes of Aramark in the world's biggest market.

Built on mutual confidence and commitment, an alliance is viable only when its terms are respected by all parties, as was the case in the Netherlands and the U.S. But during an acquisition process, how does one assess the managers' willingness to help make the combination succeed? "In our businesses, the long-term success of a subsidiary is directly proportional to the deep-seated respect for the group's values and the ambition, courage and confidence of the person in charge. Unfortunately, the buyers in an acquisition do not usually have the opportunity to audit the managers and management practices of the acquired company," underscores Bellon.

Sodexho would be faced with a disappointing experience in the case of Gary Hawkes, who, while in office, opposed some of the changes sought by Sodexho. The situation reached its peak in 2000: after being named to the group's Board of Directors by Bellon, Hawkes left the company and moved to competitor Aramark in the U.K., leaving Bellon feeling betrayed. Hawkes's course of action was also viewed as a betrayal by some of the Gardner Merchant staff, whose interests he had claimed to represent.

In 1994, the opportunity also arose to join forces with Partena, the Scandinavian food services leader. Once again, Sodexho's managers did not hesitate. They had been closely following the company's evolution and saw that Sodexho's competitors were eager to pounce.

Following negotiations led by Rémi Baudin, today vice chairman of Sodexho's Board of Directors, an agreement was signed in late December 1995. "Partena has decided to team up with Sodexho to develop its activities in Scandinavia," a December 20 press release announced to the financial community. "After considering several possibilities, Partena's shareholders and managers chose Sodexho as the best solution for developing its activities. This decision was based on the following reasons: the companies benefit

Partena

Logo, 1994

Kelvin, Gardner Merchant's specialized remote-site management subsidiary

from a highly complementary geographic distribution, offer a similar range of services, are both dedicated to delivering the highest level of quality to clients and customers, maintain the same level of commitment to training and employee motivation, and have stable shareholding bodies that share the same values."

By joining forces with Partena, which had revenues of 400 million euros and 14,000 employees, Sodexho had found a powerful ally for its Finnish subsidiary, Polarkesti, the "Little North Star," in a region where low market penetration in outsourced services bode well for future development prospects.

In 1995, Sodexho also joined forces with Universal Ogden, the American leader in remote sites, alongside Kelvin, Gardner Merchant's remote-site subsidiary, to form a new joint venture, Allied Support. Created with the aim of dominating the remote-site industry in the former USSR, Allied Support would also allow Sodexho to develop its portfolio of American clients.

Betting on North America

Sodexho's alliances with Gardner Merchant and Partena marked the start of a new era in many ways.

While continuing to pursue the organic growth that had driven the company's development from the outset, Pierre Bellon realized that for the group to maintain and strengthen its global leadership position it would also have to pursue external growth. In an increasingly consolidated market, he was fully aware that there were other outstanding opportunities to be pursued. If Sodexho did not seize them first, one of its American or U.K. competitors would.

Formulated during the union with Gardner Merchant, the alliance philosophy embodied Sodexho's response to the increasingly consolidated, globalized marketplace. It also lay behind the decision to change the group's name and logo, 30 years after their creation. From now on, all of the group's employees and businesses would be united under the Sodexho Alliance banner.

"The international working group responsible for developing the new logo decided to draw upon the existing logos of Sodexho, Gardner and Partena," explains Clodine Pincemin, group executive vice president,

OUR ALLIANCE PHILOSOPHY

Sodexho's growth is driven by the motivation and skills of its people. We may be able to buy factories, equipment, processes and technology, but the commitment, intelligence and hearts of a company's employees are not for sale. Our experience in pursuing external growth has taught us to respect the history, culture and personality of each man and woman joining our ranks. This is the underlying philosophy that has governed our most recent alliances and will continue to guide us in the future.

Sodexho
ALLIANCE

Sodexho

Gardner
Merchant

Partena

"Combining blue, red and white.
A circular movement. Five stars for
an international presence...
and first-rate service."

Communications and Sustainable Development. "This seemed to be the most appropriate approach, as the resulting logo would truly embody our alliance."

Sodexho's pursuit of alliances had just begun. In 1998, the group joined forces with Marriott Management Services (MMS), the top-ranked player in the American food services market. Once again, things moved quickly as Sodexho doubled in size for the second time in three years.

"We cannot pass up this once-in-a-lifetime opportunity to join forces with Marriott Management Services," declared Bellon. In so doing, the group followed the same line of reasoning that led it to team up with leaders in the U.K. and Swedish markets: if Sodexho did not seize the opportunity, one of its competitors would, thereby threatening its market position. But what was really at stake in the group's last major acquisition of the 20th century was its future in the American market. As the fourth-ranked player, Sodexho was still not at the same level as its competitors Aramark and Marriott, both four times bigger in terms of revenue. The only path for Sodexho was to ally itself with a major American player.

With a long, prestigious heritage dating back to 1939, Marriott Management Services had, over the course of 20 years, become the top-ranked company in the U.S. food and management services industry through an aggressive strategy of external growth. Among its major triumphs were the acquisitions of Saga in 1986, the market benchmark in education food services in the U.S., and healthcare services company United Health Services a few years later.

Begun in mid-1996, negotiations lasted more than a year and came to an end in the fall of 1997 with the official announcement of the merging of Sodexho's North American activities and Marriott Management Services under the Sodexho Marriott Services name. Sodexho would hold 47% of the venture, and Marriott International shareholders would own the rest. "Negotiations were tough," recalls Bellon. "But when we signed the deal and I shook hands with Bill Shaw, president of MMS, I felt his emotion. MMS was like a child to him."

The North American leader, with 100,000 employees and revenues of 3.7 billion euros, Sodexho Marriott Services was officially launched on March 27, 1998. The event meant that Sodexho Alliance was now earning 88% of its revenue outside France, 48% of it in the U.S. But at least as significant as the change in the group's size was the growing importance of its

Sodexho Marriott Services was officially created on March 27, 1998...
and listed on the New York Stock Exchange three days later

Sodexho's Revenues by Region

	Before MMS fiscal year 1998	After MMS fiscal year 1999
North America	34%	48%
United Kingdom and Ireland	22%	17%
Other European Countries	18%	17%
France	16%	12%
Latin America	5%	3%
Africa/Asia-Pacific	5%	3%

American subsidiary, which now accounted for half of all employees. This marked a major milestone in the evolution of the group's corporate culture.

Although the alliance looked good on paper, making it work was another matter. "Sodexho Alliance's charismatic CEO, Pierre Bellon, has taken a chance, as he is fond of doing," cautioned one article in the French business press. The two companies shared a similar client-oriented approach to their daily business, but on a broader scale their corporate cultures were very different. Marriott Management Services was a national institution in the United States, whereas Sodexho was a swashbuckling pioneer that had planted its flag in 70 countries around the world.

Both parties soon discovered that merging these two cultures would not be easy. For the employees of Sodexho North America and its CEO, Michel Landel, it would be a difficult adventure that would have an impact on the subsidiary's development.

Of course, the situation was quite out of the ordinary in more ways than one. Not only was Sodexho four times smaller than the group in which it was investing, but it was to be a minority shareholder, leaving the management of the new entity in the hands of the Marriott Management Services CEO.

According to the alliance agreement, Chuck O'Dell, CEO of Marriott Management Services, would become CEO of Sodexho Marriott Services. Under his direction, the alliance quickly abandoned the notion of partnership in favor of an outright acquisition. O'Dell would immediately place his own employees in key positions, while Michel Landel, former CEO of Sodexho's North American operations, was appointed to run the group's Canadian operations and laundry services activity. Symbolic of the difficulties encountered during the first months of the alliance, the move left Sodexho employees feeling snubbed. Within a few months, many of Sodexho's former senior managers left and the new management team imposed MMS's processes throughout the merged company, even doing away with the highly successful purchasing system implemented by Landel.

Soon after its launch at the end of 1998, Sodexho Marriott Services was coming apart, and its share price had plunged 50% on the New York Stock Exchange. During an intense meeting of the company's Board of Directors, Bellon minced no words: he felt that O'Dell was not the right person to manage the group. His demand for a replacement was supported by Edouard de Royère, honorary chairman of Air

Tony Alibrio

Bill Hamman

George Chavel

Liquide and a member of both Sodexho Alliance's and Sodexho Marriott Services' Boards of Directors, and by Bernard Carton, senior executive, Finance, Sodexho Alliance. Led by Dan Altobello, also a Sodexho Marriott Services Board member, a selection committee comprising three directors was entrusted with the mission of finding a replacement for O'Dell. It identified three internal candidates: Tony Alibrio, president, Healthcare; Bill Hamman, president, Campus Services; and Landel, who had been named president of the business and industry division a few months earlier. With the endorsement of the two other candidates, Landel was unanimously elected CEO of the company.

"Our alliance with Marriott Management Services represented the most difficult cultural challenge Sodexho had ever faced," says George Chavel, president, U.S. Healthcare. "Of course, emotional considerations must always be taken into account during a merger, but that situation marked a real turning point for the group. Not only had we become the top-ranked player in the U.S. and strengthened our leadership position worldwide but, more importantly, we managed to do so without affecting our clients."

SODEXHO FOCUSES ON FIGHTING HUNGER

Driven by its desire to make a difference in the communities where it operates, Sodexho USA launched the STOP Hunger program in the spring of 1996. "STOP" was an acronym for **S**odexho **T**eams **O**ur **P**eople, reflecting the program's capacity to focus everyone on the common goal of fighting hunger. Today, teams from all 50 states in the U.S. continue to join with customers, clients, suppliers and community members to help the 35 million Americans who go hungry every day. Activities include volunteering, fundraising and food donation programs. In 2000, Sodexho in Canada launched the STOP Hunger program, matching the U.S. in commitment and successful establishment of the program, dedicated to fighting hunger and malnutrition. (More information can be found at www.sodexho.com)

Upon becoming CEO on May 3, 1999, Landel built a new management team, reinstated the group's purchasing system, and dedicated his efforts to developing and improving the performance of the North American subsidiary. It would not be until 2001, with Sodexho's acquisition of the remaining shares in Sodexho Marriott Services, that the latter would become a fully owned subsidiary of the group.

It had taken only a little more than a decade for Pierre Bellon's American dream to come true. As he had promised the employees of Food Dimension Inc. in 1986, Sodexho had indeed become the American

STOP HUNGER

---

market leader. The realization of its founder's dream was more than just symbolically significant; it marked a major milestone in the history of the group, one that continues to have an effect to this day.

A sign of the times, and in recognition of the group's economic and financial success, Sodexho Alliance joined the ranks of the 40 leading stocks listed in the Paris Stock Exchange's CAC-40 index in May 1998. That same year, Bellon received the Chaptal of Industry business award for entrepreneurial, innovative leadership from France's National Organization for the Promotion of Industry, after having been named Manager of the Year the previous year. Despite being showered with praise and awards, Bellon maintained his legendary sense of humor, his feet firmly on the ground. "All these awards have put me on my guard," he confided to his most-trusted senior executives. "Sometimes that's all it takes to cause the performance of a company to plummet."

Sodexho's Latest Growth Initiatives

Sodexho pursued its last major external growth initiative in 2001. In 1998, the Abela group, one of Sodexho's biggest competitors in Saudi Arabia in the 1970s, decided to sell off its full range of activities following the death of its founder, Albert Abela. Sodexho was most interested in acquiring Sogeres, the fourth-ranked French food services player, which had an excellent reputation and a prestigious client roster, and Wood Dining Services, the sixth-ranked American player, operating in 20 states. As usual, Sodexho had to overcome a challenge by U.K. company Compass but managed to sign agreements with both Sogeres and Wood Dining Services thanks to the relationships it had built with the management teams of both companies.

"Sogeres and Wood Dining Services are culturally very similar to Sodexho," observed Bellon upon closing the deal. "These acquisitions will allow us to reinforce our global leadership position in the food and management services industry and our top position in the fastest growing sectors: healthcare, seniors and education." In France, it was decided that Sogeres would maintain its own name and pursue its development by positioning itself differently from Sodexho.

In 2001, Sodexho acquired the remaining 53% capital in Sodexho Marriott Services and renamed the company Sodexho, Inc. The group's positioning would remain unaltered, but this event would reinforce the cohesion of the group by uniting all of its employees under the Sodexho Alliance banner.

A Sodexho subsidiary
since 2001

Peri Bridger

Siân Herbert-Jones

The news was received with equal enthusiasm on both sides of the Atlantic. "It was a major victory for our North American employees," recalls Peri Bridger, senior vice president, Human Resources, North America. "During the transition period, we stood to benefit, both internally and externally, from associating our group with Marriott. But the fact that Sodexho Marriott Services had become a fully-owned subsidiary under the Sodexho brand would contribute greatly to the integration process."

"It was a necessary step for Sodexho to become a truly global group at all levels," affirms Siân Herbert-Jones, group chief financial officer. "These acquisitions marked a crucial turning point for the group. As that phase of external growth came to an end, we would embark on a rapid learning process in globalization."

12

An Obsession
with Organic Growth

The years when Sodexho pursued an accelerated external growth strategy were an exception in the group's history. As committed to organic growth as ever, the group would continue to enter new markets and, far from center stage, reinforce its positions in the service voucher and card and remote-site markets.

At the same time, the group was hard at work adapting its policies and organizational structures to face the challenges presented by its expansion and higher visibility.

More than ever, with the turn of a new century and a gloomy economic environment, Sodexho would need to hone its sales skills and rally its troops around the core values that had led to its success.

"The facilities management offering was a return to Sodexho's roots."

A dinner celebrating the Japanese
joint venture, 1994

A Rainbow of Cultures and Services

As Sodexho's galaxy continued to grow, the group expanded its activities into many countries, big and small.

The group launched activities in South Africa shortly after the establishment of a new political regime and the abolition of apartheid, participating in Nelson Mandela's school feeding initiative within the framework of the new South Africa's Reconstruction and Development Program. In the fall of 1998 and 1999, respectively, the group launched Sodexho Pass and food and management services subsidiaries in Tunisia, and then entered the Moroccan market.

The beginning of the new millennium would see Sodexho enter Greece, Portugal and Denmark, extending its network of major European countries.

The group also set its sights on another emerging market, the continent of Asia. Active in South Korea since 1991 via a remote-site management contract, the group launched a joint venture in Japan in 1994, partnering with two local players. During the mid-1990s, Sodexho also made its first foray into China.

To prepare Sodexho for its entry into the Chinese market, Pierre Bellon sought the advice of Michel Jan, a specialist in East Asian history and an expert on the evolution of the region's strategic, political, economic and social situation, especially where China was concerned. In June 1993, Jan organized an information day for Sodexho's senior management, and in December of that same year he accompanied Bellon on a 12-day visit to China. The decision to initiate the group's activities there was made upon their return to France. "We are investing in the next 25 years," announced Bellon upon the group's 1995 launch in China. Reflecting Sodexho's commitment to the fast-growing Asian market, a dedicated management team was formed in 1998 to oversee all of the group's operations in the region.

Patrick Poireau

The mission of developing the group's business in what would one day represent the world's largest consumer market was entrusted to Patrick Poireau, who would eventually become president, Asia/Australia Food and Management Services, after serving as managing director, Food and Management Services, Saudi Arabia. He was soon scouting out new opportunities in a region where only the most determined companies can hope to succeed.

Sodexho's teams in eastern, northern and southern China

After contemplating entry into the Vietnamese market but deciding that its current potential was insufficient to warrant the launch of a subsidiary, Sodexho headed to Guangzhou, where French auto manufacturer Peugeot had a factory. It was truly a time of adventure and discovery, without the customary market studies. When the Peugeot factory shut down, Sodexho moved on to Shanghai, fast becoming the country's commercial center. In 1995, the city was undergoing an enormous transformation. The entire region was being built from the ground up, with new urban highways, a subway system, housing, hotels, shopping malls and the new Pudong business center.

In the beginning, things were anything but easy, and visiting the kitchens of local companies proved to be a real adventure for the Sodexho team. The most complicated part was the legal aspect: even if the team managed to sign contracts, how would it go about launching the company? The only option allowed by the Chinese government was to create a joint venture, which is what Sodexho did, becoming the first global services company to obtain permission to enter the Chinese market.

During the long months of negotiations with potential Chinese partners, Sodexho called on foreign companies with offices in the region, but without much luck. Then one day, the team learned that an American international school was about to open in Shanghai. As schools always need service providers, the team knew that if it won the school's food services contract and made the students happy, it could then call on their fathers, who headed international companies in China, and say to them, "Sodexho is feeding your children. We can do the same for your companies." Sodexho's first client in China, a small school with about 100 students, paved the way for rapid growth and, two years later, the group was operating throughout eastern China. Today, the group employs nearly 10,000 people and delivers services in more than 30 cities.

Neil Barrett

In Australia, where Sodexho had launched operations in the mid-1990s with mixed results, the group benefited from the implementation of a new growth strategy initiated in early 2000. Headed by Neil Barrett, the Australian subsidiary was once again profitable with growing revenues and was able to create a solid foundation for its activities, especially in the defense segment.

"We've always been seen as the Club Med of the remote-site industry."

Having expanded its presence to 70 countries around the globe, Sodexho was able to offer its clients access to a powerful, peerless international network. From the high mountain plains of the Andes to Marseilles and Madrid, from Beijing to Washington, D.C., the group seamlessly spread its offering across regions and continents, building expertise through an intimate familiarity with local cultures.

Faced with the challenges of globalization, many companies found it necessary to focus on their core business, regardless of their size. The practice of out-sourcing was gaining momentum, with companies increasingly turning to third-party service providers for information technology, services, payroll, building maintenance and housekeeping, as well as professional training and reception services.

Given its mission of improving the daily lives of its clients, it was only natural that Sodexho continued to expand its services, which in turn allowed it to pursue organic growth. In the late 1990s, Sodexho developed a facilities management offering; in reality, however, it represented a return to the company's roots. After all, as early as 1967 it was the group's ability to offer a full range of services that enabled it to win a contract with the CNES, France's space agency, in French Guiana. Facilities management expertise had also

SOUTH AMERICA: AT THE FOREFRONT OF FACILITIES MANAGEMENT

The South American market, where the facilities management offering provided 21% of Sodexho's revenues in fiscal year 2005, is highly representative of the group's new orientation.

A benchmark in the local facilities management market, the Colombian subsidiary adopted – from its launch in the mid-1990s – a deliberate approach based on recruiting specialized engineers and working closely with its clients to develop specific tools. Today, facilities management services represent 54% of the company's revenues in Colombia.

In a region where employee mobility and knowledge sharing are common practice, it didn't take long for the group's other subsidiaries to follow suit with great success, despite competition from Compass, Aramark and the major American facilities management companies. Today, the facilities management offering represents 29% of Sodexho's revenues in Venezuela and 27% in Peru.

been accruing since the early days of the remote-site business – "We've always been seen as the Club Med of the remote-site industry," laughs Pierre Bellon – and then constantly enhanced over the years with new know-how acquired in various market segments. In the mid-1980s, for example, Sodexho was the first to offer the healthcare segment comprehensive service solutions that have since made it the world's undisputed market leader.

Sodexho's South American Executive Committee, Rio de Janeiro, 2004

Service vouchers from Argentina, Belgium, Germany, Hungary, India, Italy, Mexico and Venezuela

Not everyone in the group wholeheartedly supported the group's new facilities management positioning. Employees feared it might detract from the group's image and mission, and analysts in the financial community were quick to interpret the shift as a risky move.

But far from being a diversification, facilities management was seamlessly aligned with Sodexho's strategic commitment to improving the quality of daily life. As a result, people began to get the message, especially since it appealed to a growing number of clients. By 2000, for example, facilities management services represented 15% of consolidated revenues, and up to 30% in such markets as Colombia and Russia. In fiscal year 2005, 21% of worldwide revenues came from these end-to-end solutions, which can now comprise as many as 80 services.

Sodexho Service Vouchers and Cards

The creation of the Sodexho Pass brand in 1995 marked the start of a new era in the development of the group's service voucher and card operations. "The brand allowed us to more effectively integrate this

A MATCH MADE IN HEAVEN: NEW TECHNOLOGIES AND SODEXHO PASS

From electronic ordering systems to personalized data treatment software, IT and the service voucher industry were always well matched, as confirmed by the advent of the Internet and the new information technologies of the 1990s.

Beyond facilitating client relations and the management of activities on a daily basis, the Internet was becoming an increasingly important tool for development and dialogue. By 1997, an intranet network linked Sodexho Pass teams in the 20 markets where its services were offered. Customized to meet local linguistic and cultural needs, the network provided a forum for exchange on organizational issues and a means of resolving specific challenges. As soon as a problem was raised in a country, all of the Sodexho Pass teams were called upon to share their experiences and to find the most appropriate solution. This approach to finding solutions through online dialogue would be further advanced by the group in 2000 with the implementation of an online ordering system.

activity into the group and make our image more coherent," remembers Clodine Pincemin, group executive vice president, Communications and Sustainable Development. "But more than anything, the new name represented a break with the traditional 'paper' and 'food services' aspects of our business. Under the Sodexho Pass brand, we were able to position ourselves

STRAIGHTAWAY!

The Czech Republic, in the fall of 1997: Sodexho Czech Republic was tied for the leadership position in the service voucher market. One Friday afternoon, Didier Sandoz, managing director of the subsidiary at the time, learned that a few competitors had made offers to acquire the fourth-ranked local player, Premi Gastro. He immediately called to request a meeting with the head of the company, who responded, "You'd better act quickly, because we've received an offer that we plan to finalize on Tuesday morning."

The two men met that same evening and their conversation, confidential in tone, would evolve into a negotiation, during which Sandoz outlined an offer. With only the weekend to secure the support of Sodexho Pass's senior management, Sandoz quickly got to work. Pierre Henry, director, Central Europe, arrived on the scene the following morning and Albert George, COO, Sodexho Pass, signed off on the deal by telephone from India! By Monday morning, all of the legal documents were ready and the deal was signed at noon.

Didier Sandoz

ahead of the competition with a range of new technologies and new service offerings, building on our mission to improve the quality of daily life. This combination is the future of our business."

Under this new identity, the Sodexho Pass offering was extended to include a wider range of services and expanded into new markets. With 4.5 million users worldwide, it would represent a growing share of the group's results.

Sodexho's 1996 alliance with third-ranked Brazilian service voucher issuer Cardapio enabled it to gain a foothold in what was at the time the world's biggest service voucher market, where it would begin testing a new memory card system in 1997. Beyond offering a higher level of security, the memory card also addressed specific client needs, including the management of information flows.

The launch of a subsidiary in Bombay marked the beginning of Sodexho Pass operations in Asia. "It was a fascinating, challenging experience," recalls Albert George, then president and COO, Service Vouchers and Cards. "We were faced with one obstacle after another, including the complex nature of the market, the fact that India was a developing nation and the country's complicated administrative processes. But our determination would pay off and, blessed with a highly talented, motivated team of local employees, we would manage to diversify our service offering."

The group launched its food and management services operation in India, placing it under the supervision of

Service vouchers from India, Romania and the Czech Republic

A restaurant card in China,
where Sodexho was the first company
to obtain a license to issue such means
of payment

the country's head of service voucher and card operations, an arrangement unique in Sodexho's worldwide organization. This was followed by accelerated development of the group's facilities management offering in India in 2004 and 2005.

Begun in 1993, Sodexho Pass's expansion into Eastern Europe continued with the launch of activities in the Czech Republic in 1997 and in Poland and Slovakia in 1998.

The group's service voucher and card operations enjoyed 20% organic growth at the turn of the new century, largely due to a strategic focus on developing an innovative offering and a controlled approach to entering new markets. As the second-ranked player worldwide, Sodexho was gaining ground on market leader Accor, its historic rival; within only 15 years, the close rivalry between the two companies had helped Sodexho increase its market share relative to Accor from 0% to 75%.

In 1999, thanks to information gathered from a most unusual source (see box), Sodexho Pass led the way into the Romanian market, subsequently developing its operations elsewhere in the region. The same year, the group launched its service voucher and card operations in China, where it had had a presence since 1995, garnering its first victories in Shanghai.

TUNING IN

Sodexho owed the launch of its service voucher and card operation in Romania to the most unusual of circumstances. While installing a kitchen in the home of one of Sodexho's Paris employees, a Romanian kitchen-fitter mentioned that he had heard Accor was thinking of entering the Romanian market. Quickly informed of the news, Sodexho Pass head Albert George immediately sought confirmation in Bucharest. He learned that Accor was indeed at hand in the local market and was lobbying the government to implement regulations regarding the granting of food vouchers to company employees.

Without missing a beat, Sodexho initiated its own market study to investigate market-entry possibilities and then contacted local unions, the Ministry of Finance and the local business-lobbying group, as well as assigning full-time project responsibility to a development manager. Sodexho participated in the creation of a legal framework under which Romanian companies could grant food vouchers to their employees. The local government rewarded the efforts of the two companies by granting them the first licenses to issue vouchers in the country.

After a market study revealed that the use of vouchers was forbidden in China, Sodexho Pass leveraged modern-day technology to launch its services via an electronic "restaurant card." This made Sodexho the first company to be licensed by the city to issue smart card vouchers.

The year 1999 saw the highly symbolic entry into the U.K. market, where meal vouchers began. In the early 1980s, the group had considered acquiring long-standing player Luncheon Vouchers but decided against it because at the time, the related tax incentives were not very attractive, casting a cloud over the company's prospects. But a great deal had changed over two decades and the market had opened up to new services. Accor, which had acquired Luncheon Vouchers and built up a solid operation in the market, had become a thorn in Sodexho's side.

In October 1999, however, Sodexho was presented with an opportunity to enter the market, proving that good things come to those who wait. In its search for a supplier of service vouchers to refugees seeking asylum, the British Home Office launched a bidding process. A supplier had to be chosen before Christmas, so the bidding process kicked off a race against time. Within 48 hours, Sodexho created an international project team led by Albert George. The ten team members, including U.K. managers from the group's food and management services subsidiary as well as German, Belgian, Brazilian and

PLAYING IT SAFE ON OIL RIGS

Hygiene and safety have always been major priorities for Sodexho on all the remote sites to which it provides services. To this day, it is a market leader in this area. Sodexho's expertise has been recognized by its clients in the oil industry on several occasions. In 2004, it received an award from the International Association of Drilling Companies for its contribution to applying and maintaining hygiene and safety procedures on oil rigs off the coast of the U.K. and Ireland in the North Sea. It was the second time that Sodexho had received the recognition, which had traditionally been awarded to oil companies.

French managers from the group's respective service voucher subsidiaries, worked hand-in-hand over the following two months.

On December 20, 1999, Sodexho won the contract, as well as a victory over Accor's U.K. subsidiary in the service voucher market. The first "asylum voucher" was printed and delivered to the Home Office on April 3, 2000.

Socat, a Universal Sodexho subsidiary in Oman, receives an award in 2001 for respecting safety regulations and for four years of operation without any accidents

Universal Sodexho

The Antamina Mining Company in Peru's Andes Mountains, where Sodexho employs more than 600 people

Aside from exploring new markets to enter, Sodexho would also strengthen its position as the second-ranked service voucher player worldwide by diversifying its offering and providing vouchers for an ever-growing range of services, including food, meals, uniforms, cultural activities, sports, training and development, employment and home services. Today, Sodexho delivers more than 25 different types of service to 320,000 clients and 14 million end-users. In fiscal year 2005, the business generated 280 million euros in revenues (fees and financial income), but issue volume (number of service vouchers and cards multiplied by their face value) totaled 5.3 billion euros, giving a clearer indication of its true size.

Remote Sites

A melting pot of the group's diverse expertise, Sodexho's remote-site segment was ready to face the new century 30 years after the height of the oil rush, thanks to a diverse offering limited only by the needs of its clients. In 1999, after acquiring its American competitor, Universal Services, the remote-site division adopted the Universal Sodexho name, under which it now offers services on a global basis. That same year, following the certification of its Mexican client Pemex, Sodexho became the world's first remote-site services provider to receive ISO 9002 certification.

In South America, Sodexho also won a highly symbolic contract in Peru, where one of the world's biggest mines was being built. Nearly 14,000 feet above sea level in the Andes Mountains, construction would involve the drainage of a lake and take more than two years, employing nearly 5,000 workers. Sodexho's approach to this contract was guided by the group's principles of sustainable development.

Some 95% of the group's 650 employees in Antamina were Peruvian, 35% of them from rural communities in the region. Sodexho helped its client, the Antamina Mining Company, open a school where teams could learn about basic food hygiene. The company's agreement with local authorities also provided for cooperation with the local farming industry, so Sodexho helped to set up cooperatives to aid farmers in better managing product sales and creating the logistics needed to run their operations. The group also played a role in the development of a trout farm launched by the local bishop. This initiative paved the way for the Xchange program, which provided

Sodexho's contribution to the development of the local economy in Peru includes helping develop this trout farm

In 2004, Sodexho received the Entrepreneur trophy for its commitment to sustainable development in Peru

economic returns to local communities and to which remote-site teams in Tanzania, Alaska, Canada and Australia also contributed.

A Service-Oriented Spirit

The small Marseilles company had come a long way from preparing its first steaks and french fries in Uncle Fernand's anchovy factory to becoming the world's top-ranked food services provider. Sodexho's successful rise was exemplary, representing the dream of many an entrepreneur to one day achieve the great leap. This was not, however, Pierre Bellon's ultimate goal. "My dream is not so much that Sodexho is number one as that it endures," he says.

Long proud of its multicultural diversity, Sodexho now faced the challenge of transforming its global reach into a powerful competitive advantage. One way was to support greater cross-fertilization among subsidiaries.

The Sodexho World Innovation Forum, which was held for the first time in 1989, played a vital role in creating and perpetuating a culture of innovation within the group by providing a forum where subsidiaries could share their most outstanding contributions.

THE 12TH WORLD YOUTH DAY:
QUALITY THROUGH INNOVATION

"The pilgrims don't have to come to us; we'll go to them." This was Sodexho's approach to food services for the 12th World Youth Day, when 600,000 pilgrims would meet in and around Paris.

To face up to this enormous challenge, a new concept was developed under the leadership of Laurent Cousin, today group senior vice president, Food Offering, R&D, Food and Management Services. Meals would be distributed to and shared among groups of six pilgrims via a network of 350 mobile restaurants, each equipped with giant frying pans and capable of serving between 800 and 1,600 people. Beyond serving meals, the concept and daily positioning of the mobile restaurants helped the civil authorities to manage the crowds of pilgrims and their movements throughout Paris. During the course of WYD, 1,000 Sodexho employees, including 700 site managers, would serve as volunteers, overseeing the event's food services. In serving meals, they were assisted by another 4,000 volunteers.

"The advantage of working with Sodexho is that we could rely on the group's teams and organizational structure. Moreover, the group offered a very attractive solution based on a simple, powerful theme: that of sharing food and breaking bread together," stated Bishop Dubost, president of the WYD association.

After the event, Pope John-Paul II would even request a meeting with Pierre Bellon, during which he expressed his great satisfaction and thanked the latter for Sodexho's contributions to the success of the 12th WYD.

The mobile restaurant concept, with its giant frying pans, would also be recognized at the 1997 National Innovation Forum in France and the 1998 Sodexho World Innovation Forum prior to being rolled out at international level.

INNOVATION À LA SODEXHO

At Sodexho, innovation is defined as a new offering of products and services that has never before been marketed to clients or customers, which enables the group to:

- Increase customer and client satisfaction.
- Heighten employee motivation.
- Optimize financial results.
- Improve its corporate image.

In addition, for an innovation to be deemed successful, it has to have been implemented in a real-life context for at least six months and must demonstrate measurable profitability.

As one of the group's global objectives from the 1970s on, innovation always played a central role for Sodexho. "We knew that our ability to innovate was a key factor in our growth and ability to increase our margins," explains Michel Dubois, one of the driving forces behind the group's implementation of organized innovative processes. "Our constant pursuit of innovation manifested itself in spontaneous, sometimes anarchic ways. It took some time before we understood that in order to be more efficient, we needed to put in place an organized process to foster continuous innovation. Little by little, as the spirit of innovation was adopted by the group's subsidiaries, they were able to develop new offerings in each sector of activity." Every department contributed – from purchasing and sales to operations and communications.

Sodexho's approach was so successful that its competitors tried to take credit for some of the innovative food services concepts invented by the group. This situation necessitated the creation of the group's innovation and research department to implement protective measures, including the Sodexho Guide to Protecting Innovation.

Following the Finnish model, the group's World Innovation Forum was complemented by national forums held annually, starting in 1997. Their goal was to strengthen movement at the national level and create more opportunities for the group's talented people to express themselves. Given the group's size, the worldwide forums alone were no longer sufficient as they could not possibly cover all the innovations explored by the various divisions and innovators around the globe.

In 2003, an international study of the group's innovation processes carried out among a representative sample of 525 employees led to a new policy stressing the implementation of a small number of innovations with the potential for development in several markets. As in the industrial world, these innovations would first be tested on a limited number of sites to measure their benefits for the client as well as their profitability, ensuring that they merited the necessary investments.

"Rather than ranking number one, our goal is to be the benchmark where our customers are concerned."

Meeting client and customer needs around the globe

THE FRENCH ATOMIC ENERGY COMMISSION AND SODEXHO: 40 YEARS OF PARTNERSHIP

In 1966, the year it was launched, Sodexho signed one of its first contracts with the French Atomic Energy Commission (CEA) in Pierrelatte, and 40 years later the two parties still work closely together, with Sodexho providing services to 14 CEA sites, including the most recent Cadarache site in southern France. This exemplary relationship of trust depends solely on the quality of Sodexho's services. "Our clients are extremely demanding in terms of product and service quality. We must constantly challenge ourselves to meet their demands," underscores Yann Coléou, president, France Food and Management Services. Sodexho owes its success to its ability to position itself as a true partner and to be proactive in pursuing new ideas and solutions.

Quality was a fundamental part of Sodexho's heritage, as the group demonstrated time and again. After all, Pierre Bellon's goal from the very beginning was to improve the quality of meals served in a corporate setting.

At every major turning point in its history, including the alliances with Gardner Merchant, Partena and Marriott Management Services, Sodexho has reaffirmed this guiding principle, exemplified by its goal to set the standard of quality for its clients and customers. This is a vast undertaking, at a time when the group is a truly trans-national organization with a growing range of clients, whose expectations are becoming increasingly diversified. It is also a major challenge for a multicultural enterprise in the services industry. With hospitality practices varying widely from Norway to Japan to the Middle East, client and customer satisfaction is the only real common denominator.

In the mid-1990s, each of the group's subsidiaries was dedicated to the pursuit of quality via quality action plans, quality guarantees and, in some cases, ISO 9002 certification. From Brazil to Germany, from the Netherlands to Australia, Sodexho's quality measures spread around the globe.

In 1996, Pierre Bellon set a new challenge for the group's employees: to improve the level of perceived quality. "The notion of quality is meaningless in a void; rather, we have to consider the constantly evolving context in which our clients express and seek to meet a need," he explained. "We can, however, define perceived quality, which can be measured by how well our clients believe that we have met their expectations."

The creation of "worldwide market champion" positions in the healthcare, education and business & industry segments would also be a major step in bringing together the group's expertise at the global level. "Our job is to facilitate," proclaimed Jean-Michel Dhenain, worldwide market champion, Healthcare. One of the goals of this initiative was to identify best practices and the most valuable knowledge where the group's offering and development were concerned. As the group grew and became more complex, it also intended to introduce a cross-divisional approach that would allow for ongoing exchanges between teams and improved responsiveness.

Sodexho would undergo a technology revolution, leveraging new information and computer technology via electronic data interchange (EDI), marketing information systems, management information systems,

"We cannot improve anything that cannot be measured."

Elisabeth Carpentier

reporting systems, and Internet servers to facilitate synergies that would guarantee its cohesion and optimize business processes. Sodexho was the first food services company in France to implement an information system for real-time data interchange with suppliers, even as it successfully harmonized the parameters of a group-wide IT master plan.

In 1998, Elisabeth Carpentier was appointed group executive vice president, Human Resources. Between 1993 and 1998, the number of Sodexho employees had increased by a factor of 4.5, and while the steady string of acquisitions had considerably enhanced the group's diversity, they had also been a source of disruption in a corporate community whose members had, in a way, grown up together.

As a result, the group faced a number of human resources challenges, such as successfully integrating senior executives from newly acquired companies, developing career planning processes, dealing with the greater number of non-French managers and retaining the best employees. But the group was on familiar ground, able to draw upon the knowledge and policies developed as part of a corporate culture that had always put the highest priority on people.

"Pierre Bellon always made human resources a very high priority," recalls Carpentier. "Even at the beginning, the head of human resources reported directly to him. He took care all along to decentralize administrative aspects while centralizing the highest responsibilities of overseeing the group's human resources management. Sodexho's pursuit of external growth only highlighted the need for a human resources department at the group level to integrate our subsidiaries and anticipate needs."

Despite its profound evolution over the years, Sodexho's human resources policy was based on certain unchanging fundamental principles. "Promoting from within has been a key factor in the group's success and remains a guiding principle of our human resources policy," explains Carpentier. "By encouraging our employees to make progress and grow, and by embracing the notions of initiative and autonomy, Sodexho provides a never-ending opportunity for personal and professional development. Our human resources teams were then, and continue to be, highly focused on group employees' development to ensure that they feel proud to belong to the Sodexho community. In a difficult, little-known line of business, Pierre Bellon always sought to reinforce a feeling of belonging and pride. One of the key ways he did this

"Promoting from within has been a key factor in the group's success and remains a guiding principle of our human resources policy."

The first international employee share ownership plan

was through employee share ownership plans. Our first corporate savings plan was created in 1993. When we launched the group's first international employee share ownership plan in 2001, 19,000 employees in 22 countries, of which 90% were working on operational sites and three out of four were service employees, chose to invest in Sodexho. Today, we have more than 28,000 employee shareholders."

To meet the growing human resources demands brought on by the group's growth, Sodexho increasingly turned to external sources for recruitment while also reinforcing its management training programs. Seven years after its creation, the Sodexho Management Institute adapted to the group's growing needs by opening its doors and expanding its programs to provide annual training to 500 senior managers.

Following its alliance with Marriott Management Services, Sodexho also accelerated its rollout of a global brand policy throughout the group. This initiative owes a great deal to the determination of Clodine Pincemin, group executive vice president, Communications and Sustainable Development. The adoption of the Sodexho name by all of the group's subsidiaries from Paris to Beijing and Sao Paulo to Sydney would mark the group's advent into the era of globalization.

"For a services company like ours, branding plays a fundamental role in differentiating the organization, building customer loyalty and motivating teams," says Pincemin. "Our acquisition streak in the mid-1990s heightened this need. Having a single global brand contributed a great deal to strengthening the group's image and identity, both internally and externally. From 1995 to 1998, more than 150,000 new employees joined the Sodexho community. This new blood allowed us to rejuvenate the group, but we also had to ensure that everyone felt they were moving in the same direction and belonged to the same organization. This is where our global brand came in. Defined by Pierre Bellon when he created Sodexho, the group's values and mission represent a source of pride for everyone in the organization and are a major advantage for the company. The series of acquisitions we pursued in the mid-1990s were important in building the group's renown. In that context, implementing a global brand was a natural step, because it allowed us to strengthen and manage a coherent image for the group. Today, Sodexho is gaining recognition as a prominent international company."

Sodexho's organization continued to evolve, in line with the group's increasingly ambitious organic growth initiatives. It would, for example, organize its

From Washington to Beijing via Sao Paulo and Moscow, the group's subsidiaries have adopted the Sodexho name

"We refuse to sacrifice our future in favor of short-term results. We are not going to grow simply for growth's sake and become just another company."

clients in France, the U.K., Germany, the U.S. and many other markets according to client segment and sub-segment. In the late 1990s, a dedicated key accounts organization was created and would continually be expanded to meet the specific needs of Sodexho's major national and international clients.

Thanks to the group's dedicated efforts, organic growth led to a 7% increase in revenue for fiscal year 2000. After reaching 96% of equity in fiscal year 1998 following a period of aggressive acquisition, net debt declined to 62% in fiscal year 2001 and would drop to 27% by fiscal year 2005.

Were it not for the developing storm clouds on the horizon of the global economy, Sodexho would have been able to enjoy the benefits of its efforts. But the first signs of a sharp slowdown in the U.S. were leading most major international companies to implement drastic cost-reduction measures – including in food services, which accounted for 98% of the group's revenues. Moreover, competition in the food services market was growing more intense in the wake of the merger between Compass and Granada in 2000.

Sodexho remained determined to weather the storm. Pierre Bellon's view of the situation was unambiguous: "We refuse to sacrifice our future in favor of short-term results. We are not going to become just another company."

13

_____ **Making a Difference** _____

Fully aware of the challenges it faced, the group refused to retreat and undertook the initiatives necessary to achieve its goals. A bleak economic situation, worsened by the events of September 11, 2001, would lead the competition to engage in a merciless price war, but Sodexho would choose to take the high road, delivering professional, high quality services and creating value for clients and other stakeholders.

"When times are tough, we need to keep the attitude of a winner."

Learning to Be Global

Sodexho celebrated its 35th anniversary shortly after the turn of the new century. For many of its employees, the adventure begun in Marseilles in 1966 had lasted a lifetime.

Upon turning 70 in 2000, Pierre Bellon announced his decision to gradually step back from his operating responsibilities. Albert George, one of the group's driving forces from the very beginning and the man behind the creation and development of Sodexho's second-biggest business, service vouchers and cards, was appointed to the newly created position of group chief operating officer. The following year, he took on the responsibility of managing the group's operations worldwide, while Bellon remained chairman and CEO of Sodexho Alliance.

At the same time, Bellon decided to undertake a project to research the group's history, working with a team of historians who actively interviewed a wide range of current and past employees. Rather than write a triumphant hagiography, Bellon wanted the project to document and hand down the corporate culture and values that, brick by brick, had helped to transform a family business in a Marseilles warehouse into a global organization with more than 310,000 employees.

But the new century began dismally. The year 2001 remains inextricably linked to the September 11 attacks on the World Trade Center and the Pentagon. With 120,000 employees in the U.S. and six dining halls in the World Trade Center, Sodexho was directly affected by the catastrophe. The 46 group employees on-site at the time of the attacks demonstrated out-standing courage, and two lost their lives. In the hours following the attacks, Sodexho's American management team mobilized an emergency crisis center to assist and provide ongoing psychological support to the teams involved in the catastrophe. Sodexho's employees unanimously agree that as the tragedy unfolded, Michel Landel responded with remarkable compassion and efficiency. The group's river and harbor cruise subsidiary immediately placed its boats at the disposal of New York City authorities. Over the next several days, Sodexho's teams managed the delivery and distribution of meals to the firefighters and police officers working around the clock at Ground Zero. In the hospitals where Sodexho provided services, its employees also worked 24-hour days in an act of solidarity with the medical staff. Lastly, the entire group exhibited an unparalleled generosity through its creation of the Sodexho, Inc. Employee Disaster Relief Fund in aid of those American employees and their families who had suffered losses from the attacks.

As the economic crisis that started at the end of 2000 in the U.S. spread to Europe and the rest of the world, it was the beginning of difficult, uncertain times. Many companies, including Sodexho, would

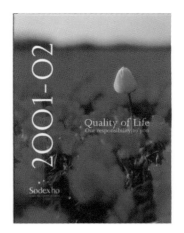

Sodexho's annual report, fiscal year 2002

be forced to adapt to harsh circumstances. At the end of 2001, Sodexho announced its financial objectives for the coming year: its goal of 3% organic growth represented only half the average level of growth it had seen over previous years, but its operating margin forecast remained stable. Its goal of reaching group net income of 210 million euros was significantly lower than market expectations of around 250 million euros. The day after the announcement was made, the group was already being penalized with an 8% drop in share price.

The first to put into perspective the often-exaggerated reactions of financial markets, which he found to be extremely short-sighted, Bellon was nevertheless not one to hide harsh realities from his employees: "Our recent success has actually harmed the group," he warned. "When things go well, people have a tendency to rest on their laurels. The group has seen average annual growth of 48% in revenues and 43% in group net income over the last 25 years, and our share price has increased by a factor of eight over the last ten years. But this outstanding performance has also led us to lower our guard where the group's efficiency is concerned." He concluded, "The current situation provides us with an excellent opportunity to speed up profitable growth and, in a more general sense, to challenge the status quo."

Sodexho found itself confronted with unprecedented challenges: upon completing a series of acquisitions representing a total investment of 4.5 billion euros, it was facing net debt representing 53% of shareholders' equity in fiscal year 2002. These figures were perfectly respectable, but the group found itself on unfamiliar ground, as it was used to high levels of significant available cash flow. Operating expenses were soaring dangerously. Hit hard by a recession in the private sector, the U.K. subsidiary was struggling and its results were weighing heavily on the group's financial figures. The new management team heading up Sodexho in the U.K. and Ireland in 2002 was looking at a long recovery period.

The group had indeed fallen into a lull. "The series of acquisitions we pursued allowed us to reinforce our global network," remembers Yann Coléou, president, France Food and Management Services. "It also taught us to approach the business differently, opening ourselves to the outside world. In France, our employees felt they had something to be proud of.

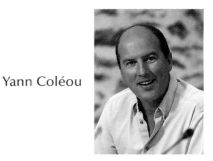

Yann Coléou

SODEXHO'S IT REVOLUTION

Becoming a truly global company, Sodexho continued to pursue the IT revolution it had begun in the mid-1990s. A structured, systematic approach was used to equip the group with the infrastructure and tools necessary to fully leverage its global synergies while also guaranteeing transparency and information sharing between its subsidiaries and sites around the globe.

As the globalization of Sodexho progressed, the group began to reevaluate its IT strategy. Sodexho created a group senior vice president, Information Technology position in October 2004, to which Philippe Taillet, CIO of Sodexho North America, was appointed. In addition, an IT Governance Committee was created to provide business oversight for IT strategy, priorities and budget. "It was the first time that IT was afforded such importance within the group," notes Taillet. "It was a significant step, which reflected the challenges facing Sodexho in terms of its information systems."

Philippe Taillet

But the flip side was that we may have lost sight of our business. When our performance began to decline, we were unprepared to respond."

That's when everyone discovered that "teaching an elephant to dance" demands patience, discipline and the courage to rethink old ways of doing things. As Bellon said: "It is much easier to bring an entrepreneurial spirit to life when starting from zero, when we launch a new subsidiary or begin a new business. This task becomes much more difficult in an organization with thousands of employees, as is the case for Sodexho in the U.S., the U.K. and France."

More than ever before, being a global company in the early 21st century meant meeting the expectations of the general public and the financial community, as they followed developments in the corporate world more closely. A growing anti-globalization movement and a rising number of serious financial scandals were creating an environment, especially in the U.S., in which the slightest mishap was severely punished. Listed on the Paris Stock Exchange as well as on the New York Stock Exchange since 2002, Sodexho, like all other major international companies, was living under the close scrutiny of the market. "We've been praised to the high heavens, which was exaggerated, and now some people are condemning us to the inner circles of hell, which is just as undeserved," is how Bellon summed up the situation.

"Our size and global presence imposed new obligations on the group, as did changes in legal requirements," underscores Siân Herbert-Jones, group chief financial officer. "Small companies can accept a certain level of risk with mainly local ramifications, but the rules of the game change when one is a listed company with a global presence and more than

"Given the group's size, we are fully aware that we need to be on guard every day against bureaucracy."

Siân Herbert-Jones

300,000 employees. We had to make sure we were carefully managing our business and counterbalancing our operations. We also had to truly embrace the notion of calculated risk at all levels of the company. From 2001 on, we revisited our financial structures and control mechanisms as part of a larger initiative to improve corporate governance, reinforcing them when necessary. But on a broader scale, our growth and regulatory requirements have given us the opportunity to improve our practices and, above all, our efficiency in managing the group."

If one word could sum up the new millennium, it would be "risk". And given the group's visibility and the nature of its business, Sodexho made a perfect target.

From food safety to environmental protection and diversity, the group's commitment to social responsibility was increasingly exposed to challenge. In 2001, the American subsidiary was accused of discriminating against the advancement of African-American employees. To avoid long and difficult legal proceedings, Sodexho, Inc. opted for a settlement with no recognition of wrongdoing by the company. The settlement was reached on April 27, 2005 and approved by the American courts on August 10, 2005. "While we believed that our case was strong, a protracted trial would have been distracting and negative for the

SODEXHO IS LISTED ON THE NEW YORK STOCK EXCHANGE

New York, April 3, 2002, 7:30 a.m.: For the stockbrokers and financiers on their way to Wall Street, it was a day like any other, but for Sodexho Alliance the day would go down in history. That morning, the group's flag proudly graced the façade of the NYSE, alongside the French and American flags. "My dream was finally coming true," confided Pierre Bellon. "That image would remain in my head as the strongest and most moving of the day."

Sodexho was being listed on the NYSE for the first time. According to tradition, Bellon rang the bell signaling the start of the trading day at 9:30 a.m., an honor bestowed on only a handful of French businessmen. Beyond the symbolic importance of the event, it would also allow Sodexho to increase its visibility in its biggest market.

"When we arrived on the floor," recalls Lisa Tripoli, one of Sodexho's 25 American chefs invited to the ceremony, "NYSE president Richard Grasso said to us, 'Don't be nervous. There are only 150 million people watching you.' When I got back to the hospital where I work, everyone had seen me on CNN. It was a fantastic day, one I will never forget."

AT THE HEART OF PUBLIC HEALTH CONCERNS

Since 1996, Sodexho had established supply channels that allowed it to verify the origin of food products and required its suppliers to abide by very strict contractual quality guidelines. To heighten its control of food-related risks, Sodexho created a scientific council of specialized, recognized nutrition and food safety experts in France in 1999. The council received technical support from the Institut Pasteur medical research center in Lille, a partner of the group for over 20 years, and AFSA, France's food safety agency. This initiative would help Sodexho implement food traceability measures and an ongoing health watch under the aegis of its purchasing quality team in France.

image of the group, especially in the U.S.," explained Rohini Anand, chief diversity officer of Sodexho North America. "Instead, our commitments and initiatives in favor of diversity and equality during the preceding several years were recognized and the legal proceedings did not have a lasting impact on our reputation."

The business community recognized Sodexho's pursuit of diversity and dedication in promoting it with numerous honors. In 2003, Michel Landel, CEO of Sodexho North America, received the Diversity Best Practices CEO Leadership Award and was named

Advocate of the Year by *Asian Enterprise Magazine* for his commitment to integrating minorities within the group. Sodexho was also recognized with the Multicultural Foodservice and Hospitality Alliance's Strategic Example of Excellence in Diversity Award, among numerous others. (A list of recognitions received by Sodexho in this area can be found in the Sustainable Development section of the group's website: www.sodexho.com.)

WE SUPPORT
THE GLOBAL COMPACT

The Winds of Change

As globalization brings unprecedented challenges, it also opens the door to new opportunities. For Sodexho, one of the most rewarding involves bringing to life its mission of "improving the quality of daily life."

Rohini Anand

Under the leadership of its new CEO, Nicolas Japy, Universal Sodexho is adapting its organization and processes to respond to the demands of the increasing globalization of the remote-site industry.

"Our core business has not changed, in that we offer no fewer than 70 different services. But the context in which we provide them has changed a great deal," explains Japy. "The market has become even more competitive and our clients are much more

Nicolas Japy

demanding. As in many other sectors, we have fewer clients, but they are bigger players. A key challenge is to increasingly anticipate changes in the market and in the needs of our clients in order to position ourselves as true partners. This is what prompted us to create a strategic market monitoring team as part of a broader approach that includes internal and external networks of contacts and information, as well as networks that bring together the group's diverse skills and expertise. This is a crucial dimension to our business and a driving force behind our competitive edge. Another major challenge we are facing, as our role as a facilities management provider becomes increasingly technical, is to build and reinforce a team of technical experts with new specialized knowledge and skills. Finally, we have acquired considerable experience in the area of sustainable development, which represents a major advantage in today's market. We continue to enrich this expertise as the governments of the countries where our clients operate place ever greater emphasis on the development of local communities when they grant permission to enter their markets."

While continuing to strengthen its position in its traditional lines of business, Sodexho was also hard at work preparing itself for the future and seeking out new client segments in defense as well as in correc-

WORKING HAND-IN-HAND WITH LOCAL COMMUNITIES

In September 2005, Sodexho was chosen by Inco to supply a full range of services to the Goro Nickel mine construction site in New Caledonia. More than 40 services ranging from laundry to entertainment would be provided to more than 4,000 people over 32 months.

As with previous projects in Peru, Alaska and Tanzania, Sodexho made local recruitment a priority, hiring New Caledonians to fill more than 95% of jobs and providing training with the help of specialized entities. But that was just the beginning. Sodexho has since helped to create micro-enterprises to supply certain services, including waste pick-up and treatment; it also provides employee transportation. Additionally, it has helped promote local produce and livestock farms to meet the construction site's needs with the goal of helping these businesses develop the structure and operations necessary to provide goods and services once the mine is opened.

tions, where the group applies its rigorous ethical standards. For correctional facilities, this means that Sodexho will only provide services in those countries that are established democracies, where the death penalty is illegal, and where priority is given to rehabilitative policies for inmates. Moreover, Sodexho does not provide services in situations where its staff would be required to carry firearms. "After France and the U.K., we developed operations in Australia and Chile, where we also offer a wide range of services,"

CORRECTIONAL FACILITIES: TREATING OTHERS RESPECTFULLY AND TEACHING RESPONSIBILITY

Sodexho delivers comprehensive solutions for correctional facilities based on a full range of services to improve living conditions and prepare inmates for constructive resettlement in society. The offering ranges from food services and logistics to total management of the facility, including security and rehabilitation support services.

Since 2000, Sodexho has provided total management and operations for Forest Bank Prison near Manchester, U.K. This project has proven that a different vision of correctional facilities is possible. "Depriving someone of freedom is in itself a punishment," states the prison director. "The moment the doors are locked behind a new inmate, we must provide everything he or she needs to successfully rehabilitate him or herself and resettle into society. Time in prison mustn't be an idle period: a custodial environment can have a positive outcome." These are the beliefs that guided all the players in the project led by UKDS, the Sodexho subsidiary in the U.K. that specializes in corrections.

To provide services to Forest Bank, for example, UKDS built a team of administrative staff and prison custody officers composed largely of employees who had never worked in the correctional business. These employees were recruited according to their interpersonal skills and dedication to improving inmates' prospects for the future and contributing to their rehabilitation. After going through preliminary training, the prison custody officers continue to attend annual seminars. Great importance is also placed on encouraging inmates to stay in touch with their families. To facilitate this approach, each inmate is asked to designate two telephone numbers that they can call free of charge while in custody. In workshops linked directly to the local economy, UKDS also makes it a priority to provide vocational training and paid employment, as well as to teach the behavioral skills necessary for resettlement.

reflects Herb Nahapiet, worldwide market champion, Correctional Services. "An increasing number of governments are turning to the private sector to improve the quality of services in correctional facilities."

In 2002, the group strengthened its position in the defense segment with the signing of its biggest contract to date, worth more than one billion dollars over eight years, for food services on Marine Corps bases in the U.S. It would also be awarded its first contract with the Swedish military. In fiscal year 2005, defense industry sales of 353 million euros accounted for 3% of the group's revenues.

Sodexho's experience in the U.K., where it benefited from the government's outsourcing policies, allowed it to build its expertise in the sector. While many NATO countries were reducing their defense budgets following the fall of the Berlin Wall, the U.K. government was one of the first in Europe to consider outsourcing support services for its armed forces.

In 1997, the U.K. subsidiary signed a contract with the Aldershot Garrison, the Center of Excellence for Army Sport, where it would head a consortium of 1,000 employees responsible for providing 42 services including cleaning, health and food services, waste disposal, secretarial services, building management and maintenance, and heating. An initial seven-year

A manual created by UKDS for detainees at the Forest Bank correctional facility near Manchester, U.K.

Herb Nahapiet

The US Marine Corps,
one of Sodexho's biggest
defense contracts

Philip Jansen

contract was extended to 2005, and in 2006 Sodexho will participate in the reconstruction and management of the new garrison. Aldershot became a model of outsourced support services, allowing the group to sign new contracts in the sector and amass expertise that would be essential in winning a 25-year contract in 2004, as part of a consortium, for the reconstruction and management of Colchester Garrison.

After going through difficult times, Sodexho's U.K. subsidiary has begun to reap the rewards of its efforts and to restore profitability to many of its business segments. "Our facilities management expertise enables us to benefit from the demand for an increasingly wide range of services in the defense, correctional and healthcare sectors," said Philip Jansen, group COO and chief executive, United Kingdom and Ireland.

More than ever before, the group remained determined to accelerate organic growth by focusing on three strategic pillars: building client loyalty, cross-selling to existing clients and winning new clients. In the words of then chief operating officer Albert George, "We have to evolve from the role of 'producers' to that of 'marketers' and 'sellers', without losing our managerial skills."

In 2003, the group began rolling out John Gamble's Clients for Life® program, which had been successfully used by the group's U.S. healthcare division since 2000.

Sodexho's client loyalty crusade was led by worldwide market champion Dick Macedonia, group COO and CEO, North America Food and Management Services, as well as by Sophie Clamens, group senior vice president, Client Relations, who was entrusted with coordinating the implementation of Clients for Life® in all the group's entities. "Our goal is to increase the group's client retention rate from 93% to over 95% within three years," she remarks. "The Clients for Life® program is remarkable in that it places emphasis on our daily interactions with our clients," declares Macedonia. "We are fully aware that this initiative represents a serious commitment and a major change in the way we do business, but it is a key factor in our growth."

"We not only need new methods, we also need to embrace the underlying spirit of the approach," adds Clamens. "We are convinced that our ability to increase client retention depends on concrete practices as well as a broader challenge more akin to a change in our corporate culture than simply attending a training course."

"Client loyalty is the driving force behind Sodexho's growth."

Richard Macedonia

Sophie Clamens

Rick Brockland

The group revisited its founding principles and strengthened its commitment to client loyalty, building upon its tradition of a client-oriented culture. Sodexho approaches client relations from the viewpoint of a partnership, which reinforces client loyalty. Thus, in the education market, "Sodexho's mission does not end at the door to the dining facility or school cafeteria," says Rick Brockland, worldwide market champion, Education, and president, Education United States Food and Management Services.

"Facing the alarming increase in obesity among young people, our clients look to Sodexho for help to address this and other significant issues. Childhood obesity, which is becoming a serious public health problem, calls for a comprehensive approach that involves all the stakeholders in the education segment.

"As the world's leading private employer of clinical dietitians, Sodexho has the expertise to help clients implement programs to educate young people about nutrition and to encourage healthy eating. Schools face complex challenges and increasing service demands with limited budgets. Sodexho tailors its integrated facilities management offering to the specific requirements of the clients' core business. In this approach, we help to optimize facility operations as well as contributing to the improvement of the community, as our successful partnership with the St. Louis School District demonstrates," adds Brockland.

After its 1996 U.S. launch, the group's STOP Hunger program was rolled out throughout the group in 2003, with a dedicated organizational structure responsible for its international development. Sodexho increased its efforts to fight against malnutrition and hunger in all forms, working hand-in-hand with major global and local charities and supporting efforts already in place.

By fiscal year 2005, STOP Hunger programs had been launched in 19 countries to fight hunger through volunteer work, training and information for hunger relief workers and underprivileged people on the benefits of a balanced diet, as well as through food and monetary donations. In each country with a developed program, a Sodexho STOP Hunger foundation or association was created to coordinate local initiatives. In the U.S., for example, the Sodexho Foundation has provided more than 5.5 million dollars to hunger relief since its inception in 1999, sponsoring and supporting programs that fight hunger and its root causes in the U.S.

SODEXHO'S COMMITMENTS TO SUSTAINABLE DEVELOPMENT[1]

...Where our clients are concerned:
"Sodexho is dedicated to creating value for its clients over the long term, thereby forging strong partnerships."

...Where our customers are concerned:
"Sodexho is dedicated to developing a portfolio of services that help improve the quality of life for everyone who has entrusted us with their well-being,...to reducing food safety risks...[and] to informing future generations about the importance of eating correctly and educating them regarding best practices."

...Where our employees are concerned:
"Sodexho is dedicated to providing its employees with a powerful 'social elevator' and to promoting and respecting diversity."

...Where our suppliers are concerned:
"Sodexho is dedicated to pursuing procurement policies that guarantee the origin of the products we use...[and] strongly encouraging its suppliers to respect its sustainable development values."

...Where our shareholders are concerned:
"Sodexho is dedicated to regularly and simultaneously providing all shareholders with the same accurate, clear, transparent information."

...Where our host countries are concerned:
"Sodexho is dedicated to supporting the development of local economies by promoting local hiring...and, in the most disadvantaged countries, local initiatives to stimulate economic growth."

"Sodexho is dedicated to expanding its program to fight malnutrition to the main countries in which it operates."

"Sodexho is dedicated to helping protect the environment in its host countries."

1. Excerpts from the 2003 Ethical Principles and Sustainable Development Contract.

At the same time in France, Sodexho's partnership with hunger relief organization Restos du Cœur (www.restosducœur.org) resulted in the distribution of 203,000 meals to the underprivileged and the training of 550 volunteers in dietary principles and food hygiene during the winter of 2005. To help foster reintegration through employment, Sodexho has committed itself to hiring operational employees from among beneficiaries of Restos du Coeur meals and training.

In January 2003, in the presence of the French prime minister, Sodexho received the Ethics and Governance Prize awarded by French newspaper *Le Figaro* for its participation in the fight against hunger. That same year, it adopted its Ethical Principles and Sustainable Development Contract, thereby formalizing its commitment in this area. Pierre Bellon placed Clodine Pincemin, a member of the Sodexho Executive Committee as well as group executive vice president, Communications and Sustainable Development, in charge. "This approach, which is the result of deep reflection on the part of everyone concerned, has confirmed and strengthened daily practices pursued by the group from the very start," she emphasizes.

DIVERSITY IN CANADA

"Our compound growth rate of more than 10% during the last decade has created 8,500 new jobs, bringing our Canadian family to over 12,000 strong," remarks Garry Knox, president and CEO, Canada. "We have worked closely to foster deep community roots. Sodexho received the PAR (Progressive Aboriginal Relations) Silver Award in 2002 and the PAR Gold Award in 2004 and again in 2006 from the Canadian Council for Aboriginal Business."

Sodexho's efforts in this area have also been recognized by the four major responsible-investment indices with the group's listing on the FTSE4Good Europe in 2001, the ASPI Eurozone in 2004 and the DJSI World and DJSI STOXX (Europe) in September 2005.

Not about to succumb to dismal market conditions or other difficulties, Sodexho started to see an upturn when its organic growth reached 4.1% in fiscal year 2004 as compared to 1.9% in fiscal year 2002. As the group returned to the path of growth, its managers realized that its recent difficulties were not solely the result of economic conditions – there was something else. The entire organization was buzzing with anxiety: What would become of Sodexho following Pierre Bellon's departure?

Sodexho's Ethical Principles and Sustainable Development Contract is translated into 14 languages

14

__ We've Only Just Begun...__

Sodexho's 40th anniversary and preparation for the arrival of a new CEO marked a major turning point in its history. But as its founder prepared to step down, his legacy and the values upon which he had built the group were certain to continue.

"My management philosophy has been influenced by my Christian upbringing," acknowledges Pierre Bellon. "I did my best to incorporate my deep-seated beliefs in respect for mankind and social equality into the group's daily business dealings."

The all-important question of who would take his place had become even more pressing with Albert George's retirement in early 2003 due to health problems. As group COO, he had been the obvious candidate to fill Bellon's shoes. Within a few months,

"Making every day a better day."

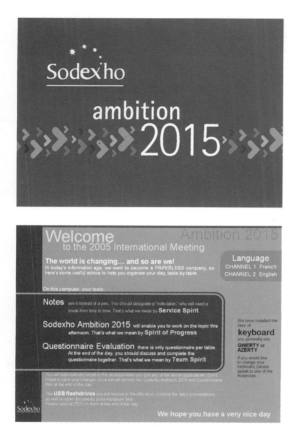

The Sodexho Ambition 2015 initiative
is presented at the group's
international meeting in February 2005

Jean-Michel Dhenain and Michel Landel were both named president and COO, with the responsibility of overseeing the group's operations worldwide. A successor had yet to be named.

As the group approached this important crossroads, the need to take stock of its orientation was evident, and, as was his custom, Bellon sought the input of the group's employees.

In 2003, the group launched the participatory Sodexho Ambition 2015 initiative. "Over the past three years, our results have not matched our ambitions and the share price has declined. This has led the Executive Committee and Board of Directors to consider whether we should change our strategy. We believe that no change in strategic direction is warranted because our current strategy provides us with four outstanding advantages for both now and the future: powerful competitive positions, a comprehensive global network, considerable growth potential and an excellent financial model. We realize that if we are not going to change our strategy to improve our future performance, then we must change in response to developments in our business environment." This is how Bellon explained the group's approach during the Annual Shareholders' Meeting held on February 8, 2005.

"Where would you like to see Sodexho ten years from now?" was the question asked of 350 senior managers. Around the world, workshops addressed the question of the group's future. The workshops' first findings revealed that there was a widespread belief in the group's values, with 93% of participating managers feeling strongly attached to them. Participants also felt closely tied to the group itself. However, there were strong expectations for change in the group's way of working. The survey also confirmed that the group's employees saw the task of finding a successor for Bellon to be a major challenge.

Starting in the fall of 2004, the group's strategic planning would take survey feedback into account according to five major strategic positions: adhering to the group's values; accelerating profitable organic growth; improving management; improving operations and operating margins; and strengthening the role of the Board of Directors and reinforcing internal controls.

The group had created its roadmap for the future.

On September 15, 2004, the group released the details of the succession process. On September 1, 2005, Bellon would hand over the reins as chief executive officer to Michel Landel, but would continue to serve as chairman of the Board. Within the group, the

Jacques Pétry

news came as no surprise; Landel was widely recognized for his outstanding leadership abilities and intimate knowledge of the group, which made him the obvious candidate to replace Bellon. As a Frenchman who had achieved great success in the U.S., he epitomized the spirit of the group.

The year-long transition period allowed the two men to work together and share their experiences, as Bellon prepared to retire and Landel prepared to assume the responsibilities of Bellon's lifelong project. It also provided time for the group to strengthen its management structure. At the end of 2005, another legendary figure, one of the group's earliest craftsmen and the driving force behind its success in the healthcare industry, Jean-Michel Dhenain, left the group. Sodexho's commitment to strengthening its management team by drawing on specialized outside resources led it to replace him with Jacques Pétry, who benefited from long experience in the service industry, with its strong human element. "Sodexho serves one of the most noble causes. I feel honored and delighted to be able to contribute to the group's mission by helping it pursue and expand its facilities management offering," remarked Pétry. "I am proud to join a civic-minded company that is aware of its obligations toward future generations."

Pierre Bellon reiterated his faith in Sodexho before its shareholders and employees: "I would like to draw together the past, the present and the future. Sodexho will soon be 40 years old. During our history, I have been Sodexho's core shareholder and chief executive. We are now entering a new period.

"Some of you may not be aware that when I created the company, I wanted it to remain independent. We have succeeded in this effort since Bellon SA today holds a roughly 39% interest in Sodexho. For more than 30 years, I have been donating shares to my four children, who today own 68% of all Bellon SA shares. They are bound by a shareholders' agreement to hold these shares, thus ensuring Sodexho's future independence.

"I firmly believe that with a stable, loyal family shareholder base and an expanded Board of Directors, Michel Landel, leading a strengthened senior management team, will oversee an era of new prosperity for our clients, our employees and you, our shareholders."

A page had turned. Sodexho was about to embark upon a new adventure.

Deeply committed to making a difference in today's world, with services that have a direct impact on our daily lives, Sodexho remains fully aware that making each day a better one is an ongoing commitment to

"I would like to draw together the past, the present and the future."

On September 15, 2004, Pierre Bellon presented the succession process

Michel Landel

be taken seriously. Diverse and independent, the global leader looks toward the future with confidence and enthusiasm, ready as ever to take on the challenges and opportunities that are sure to appear along the way.

When asked about his vision for Sodexho, Michel Landel offers that it is "making every day a better day for our clients, customers, employees, shareholders and all the local communities in our host countries. It is only through the motivation, passion and talent of every single one of our employees that we will be able to make this happen. It is a goal worthy of Sodexho's history."

2005 FISCAL YEAR

Revenues by region:

☐	North America	43%
☐	Continental Europe	35%
☐	The U.K. and Ireland	11%
☐	Africa and Asia-Pacific	7%
■	South America	4%

Revenues by activity:

—	**Food and facilities management**	**98%**
☐	Business and industry	39%
▨	Defense	3%
▨	Correctional services	2%
■	Healthcare	18%
▨	Seniors	6%
☐	Education	24%
☐	Remote sites	6%
■	**Service vouchers and cards**	**2%**

The service voucher and card operation represents 2% of group revenues and 30% of business volume. Issue volume (number of service vouchers and cards multiplied by their face value) of 5.3 billion euros more accurately represents the importance of this activity.

Internationalization

*

Clients for Life®

*

Contributing to the economic
and social development
of host countries

During this period, Sodexho's revenues grew by a factor of four, from 2.8 to 11.7 billion euros, at an average annual growth rate of 15%. Net income increased by a factor of five, from 43 to 197 million euros (excluding the litigation settlement in the U.S.), at an average annual growth rate of 16%.

Timeline (1966-2005)

FMS: Food and Management Services, today known as Food and Facilities Management Services
SVC: Service Vouchers and Cards

Year	Milestones
1966	Pierre Bellon creates Sodexho in Marseilles on March 3. First major contracts in France: the Atomic Energy Commission, including the Pierrelatte location.
1967	Sodexho's first logo, three teacups hanging in a ship's storeroom, is created. Contract with the CNES (French National Space Center) in Kourou, French Guiana.
1968	Sodexho Brazil (FMS) is launched.
1969	General management moves to Saint-Cloud, west of Paris.
1970	Sodexho Monaco (FMS) and Sodexho Belgium (FMS) are launched. Sodexho begins operations in sub-Saharan Africa (Gabon and Cameroon). A management training center is created in Marseilles.
1971	Sodexho becomes the second-ranked food services company in France.
1974	Sodexho acquires Italmense (FMS) and enters the Italian market. The fiscal year is changed to begin on September 1 and end on August 31.

1974-1975	Sodexho Spain (FMS) is launched. The Sodexho catering subsidiary is launched in Scotland to manage oil platforms in the North Sea. The first remote-site services contracts are signed in Saudi Arabia. Abbar & Zaïny/Sodexho is founded.
1975-1976	General management moves to Montigny-le-Bretonneux, southwest of Paris. Sodexho GmbH (FMS) is launched in Germany.
1976-1977	Sodexho makes its first foray into the meal voucher market with the acquisition of Chèque Repas in Belgium. Sodexho Iran and Sodexho Cameroon are launched.
1977-1978	Sodexho Norway (remote sites) is launched.
1978-1979	Sodexho Ivory Coast is founded. Sodexho launches operations in the Congo and Niger. Sodexho publishes consolidated accounts for the first time. Sodexho Boatel (remote sites) is launched in Venezuela and the Al Rubaya Sodexho Catering Company is launched in the United Arab Emirates.
1979-1980	Contract with the Atomic Energy Commission for residential services at the remote site for nuclear testing in Mururoa, French Polynesia. Sodexho Polynesia is launched.
1980-1981	Sodexho acquires Ticket Repas and enters the meal voucher market in France. Subsidiaries are launched in Niger, Nigeria, Congo and Chile (FMS).
1981-1982	Rémi Baudin is named director and group senior vice president. Sodexho's bid to take over Jacques Borel International (JBI) fails.
1982-1983	Sodexho is listed on the secondary market of the Paris Stock Exchange on March 2, 1983. Sodexho New Caledonia is created.
1983-1984	Sodexho is listed on the first market of the Paris Stock Exchange.

1984-1985	The first *Oh! Poivrier* restaurant is opened in Paris. Acquisition of Seiler's (FMS) in New England. Sodexho segments its operations in France with the creation of business, education and healthcare subsidiaries. Sodexho becomes the sixth-ranked food services company worldwide.
1985-1986	Company headquarters are moved to Montigny-le-Bretonneux, southwest of Paris. Sodexho acquires FDI (Food Dimension Inc.) in California (FMS).
1986-1987	Sodexho acquires Chèque Restaurant and Bateaux Parisiens in France. Sodexho acquires Cheque Ristorante in Italy. Sodexho acquires Crawley & McCracken (FMS) in Canada. Sodexho launches SVC operations in Luxembourg.
1987-1988	Acquisition of Western Food Enterprises, In Plant and Dietary Consultant Inc. in the U.S. (FMS). Sodexho provides residential and food services to the Winter Olympics in Calgary. SVC activities are launched in Spain.
1988-1989	Sodexho teams up with the Compagnie Internationale des Wagons-Lits. The first of seven Sodexho World Innovation Forums is held in Versailles, France.
1989-1990	SVC activities are launched in Chile. Acquisition of Prestamex in Mexico (SVC). Batobus is created in Paris. The SIGES subsidiary is created to manage five correctional facilities in France. Sodexho Prestige is created. Sodexho receives an award from the Belgian Minister of Employment for its Chèque Emploi.
1990-1991	The agreement between Sodexho and the Compagnie Internationale des Wagons-Lits comes to an end. Acquisition of Belgian companies Restaura and Belgorest (FMS). Acquisition of Eiring Catering in Germany (FMS). Acquisition of Spirit Cruises, the U.S. leader in river and harbor cruises.

1991-1992	Sodexho enters the South Korean market with a remote-site services contract. The Sodexho Management Institute (SMI) is created. Sodexho becomes the official food services provider for the Tour de France. Sodexho provides food services to the Olympic Village during the Winter Olympics in Albertville and Summer Olympics in Barcelona.
1992-1993	Sodexho begins its collaboration with rising French chef Marc Veyrat with the creation of the School for Chefs and a select club of Sodexho's top ten chefs. Sodexho launches operations in the Czech Republic (FMS) and Hungary (FMS). Sodexho enters the Scandinavian market for the first time with the acquisition of Finnish company Polarkesti (FMS). SVC activities are launched in Venezuela, Turkey, Hungary and Austria.
1993-1994	A corporate savings plan is created. An FMS subsidiary is launched in Turkey. Sodexho provides food services to the Olympic Village during the Winter Olympics in Lillehammer. FMS activities are launched in Russia and Poland.
1994-1995	Following its alliance with U.K.-based Gardner Merchant, the largest food services provider in Europe, Sodexho becomes the global market leader. The group signs its first contract in China, in Shanghai (FMS). The global Sodexho Pass brand is created for SVC operations. SVC activities are launched in the Czech Republic. SVC and FMS activities are launched in Colombia. FMS activities are launched in Japan.
1995-1996	Sodexho joins forces with Partena, Sweden's leading services provider. Sodexho invests in Brazilian company Cardapio (SVC). The STOP Hunger initiative is launched in the U.S.

1996-1997	Sodexho is renamed Sodexho Alliance.
	Following the acquisition of Universal Ogden, the North American remote-site services leader, the remote-site activity is renamed Universal Sodexho.
	Sodexho Pass makes its first foray into India.
	The first Sodexho National Innovation Forum is held in Finland.
1997-1998	Sodexho teams up with Marriott Management Services to form Sodexho Marriott Services, the leading food services company in North America, listed on the NYSE.
	Sodexho Alliance is listed in the CAC 40 index on the Paris Stock Exchange.
	Creation of Altys Multiservice, a French subsidiary specializing in facilities management.
	Sodexho handles food services for World Youth Day in Paris.
	Pierre Bellon is named Manager of the Year by international consultancy A.T. Kearney and *Challenges* magazine.
1998-1999	Global remote-site services activities are brought together under the Universal Sodexho brand.
	Sodexho Pass launches operations in Slovakia, Poland and Argentina.
	Sodexho launches operations in Peru (FMS).
1999-2000	The Sodexho name is increasingly rolled out as a global brand.
	Sodexho's website is launched.
	Sodexho handles food services for World Youth Day in Rome (1.5 million pilgrims).
	Sodexho provides food services to the Olympic Village during the Summer Olympics in Sydney.
	Sodexho Pass enters the Romanian and Chinese markets.
2000-2001	Albert George is named COO of Sodexho Alliance.
	Acquisition of Sogeres (FMS) in France and Wood Dining Services (FMS) in the U.S.
	Acquisition of 53% of Sodexho Marriott Services, making it a wholly-owned Sodexho subsidiary under the name Sodexho, Inc.
	An international employee share ownership plan is introduced.
	Sodexho Pass is launched in the U.K.

2001-2002	Sodexho launches FMS in India. On April 2, 2002, Sodexho Alliance is listed on the New York Stock Exchange. Sodexho wins a food services contract for 55 U.S. Marine Corps garrisons in the U.S. Sodexho launches FMS in Costa Rica. The International Association of Drilling Companies recognizes Sodexho's contributions to applying and respecting safety procedures on oil rigs in the North Sea.
2002-2003	Jean-Michel Dhenain and Michel Landel are named COOs of Sodexho Alliance, replacing Albert George. The STOP Hunger initiative is rolled out throughout the group. Sodexho formalizes its commitment to sustainable development with its Ethical Principles and Sustainable Development Contract. Michel Landel is one of ten American executives to receive the Diversity CEO Leadership Award.
2003-2004	Sodexho launches FMS in Thailand. Sodexho handles food services for the Rugby World Cup in Sydney, Australia. Sodexho Peru receives the prestigious Entrepreneurial Creativity Award for its Sodexho por el Desarollo Sostenible association. Sodexho Pass is launched in the Philippines and Panama. Sodexho is launched in Switzerland (FMS). Sodexho is awarded the Ethics and Governance Award by *Le Figaro* for its STOP Hunger initiative.
2004-2005	Sodexho Pass wins first contracts in Peru. Sodexho provides food services to World Youth Day in Cologne, Germany. The STOP Hunger program is rolled out in 17 countries. Sodexho Alliance is listed in two socially responsible investment indices: DJSI World and DJSI STOXX; it is the first French group to be listed as a super-sector leader in its category. On September 1, Pierre Bellon steps down from the position of CEO but remains chairman of the Board of Directors; Michel Landel is named group CEO, Sodexho Alliance.

Acknowledgments

The Sodexho Story would never have existed were it not for the dedication, collaboration, time, energy and passion of all those involved.

Our thanks go to Sodexho's women and men, present and past, for their contributions, help and desire to share their memories: Dany Abasse (France), Tony Alibrio (U.S.A.), Al Allen (U.S.A.), Rohini Anand (North America), Mary Attenweiller (U.S.A.), Patrice Aubert (France), Robert Barthélémy (France), Geraldine Bateman (U.S.A.), Rémi Baudin (Group), Yves Bayon de Noyer (Remote Sites), Astrid Bellon (Director), François-Xavier Bellon (Director), Pierre Bellon (Group), Antoine Benech (Group), Mark Bickford (U.S.A.), Rodney Bond (U.S.A.), Paul Bonnette (Group), Josette Bouveyron (France), Steve Brady (North America), Gérard Brice (Group), Peri Bridger (North America), Dominique Brillaud (France), Rick Brockland (North America), John Bush (North America), Elisabeth Carpentier (Group), Bernard Carton (Group), Eric Charrat (France), George Chavel (North America), Didier Chenet (France), Antonino Cirrincione (Brazil), Sophie Clamens (Director), Yann Coléou (France), Richard Coudyser (France), Laurent Cousin (Group), Jean-Pierre Cuny (Group), Plinio De Oliveira (Brazil), Jean-Michel Dhenain (Group), Patrice Douce (Group), André Dubloc (France), Michel Dubois (Group), Raphaël Dubrule (Group), Alain Epstein (France), André Favière (Remote Sites), Florence Fong (U.S.A.), Nigel

Forbes (U.K. and Ireland), Jean Frégnac (Group), Albert George (Group), Gilbert Gherci (Remote Sites), Claudia Guiloff (South America), Bill Hamman (U.S.A.), Pierre Henry (Vouchers and Cards), Jean Herbert (France), Siân Herbert-Jones (Group), Vincent Hillenmeyer (Group), Phil Hooper (U.K. and Ireland), Richard Hutchinson (U.S.A.), Nicolas Japy (Remote Sites), Roger King (U.S.A.), Garry Knox (Canada), Pierre Lafond (France), Ian Lamberton (U.K. and Ireland), Michel Landel (Group), Alison Lazerwitz (Group), Marie-Pierre Le Lohé (Group), Michel Lebreton (France), Michel Lorin (Group), Dick Macedonia (North America), Stephen MacManus (U.K. and Ireland), Martin MacNeill (U.K. and Ireland), Anne-Marie Maisonnave (Remote Sites), Mireille Mantion (France), James Marvin (U.S.A.), I.V. Mashburn (U.S.A.), Noël Mead (U.K. and Ireland), Teddy Megarbane (Group), Jean-Rémy Molière (France), André Monredon (France), Joe Mullane (U.K. and Ireland), Tom Mulligan (U.S.A.), Alain Neyrinck (Remote Sites), Fred O'Brien (U.S.A.), Emeka Okeani (U.S.A.), Christophe Parent (Remote Sites), Vince Pearson (U.K. and Ireland), Jacques Pétry (Group), Michelle Philpott (U.K. and Ireland), Antoine Piéri (France), Marja Lisa Pihlstrom (Group), Clodine Pincemin (Group), Kirsti Piponius (Finland), David Plant (U.K. and Ireland), Patrick Poireau (Asia), Denise Prandini (France), Michel Ravon (France), Pierre Revillon d'Appreval (Remote Sites), Hans Rijnierse (Netherlands), Peter Roberts (U.K. and Ireland), Denis Robin (Group), Pierre Sannini (France), Jean-François Sautereau (France), Christophe Solas (China), Giacomo Sorlini (Italy), Danièle Souef (Group), Bob Stern (North America), Lynne Street (U.K. and Ireland), Nathalie Szabo (Director), Philippe Taillet (Group), Susan Tatum (U.S.A.), Jacques Tavel (France), Camille Therrien (Canada), Allan Tilley (U.K. and Ireland), Damien Verdier (Group), Philippe Voraz (South America) and Bob Wood (U.S.A.).

We would like to give special thanks to Albert George, COO of Sodexho Alliance and chairman of the Executive Committee from 2000 to 2002, for gathering and summarizing information on the group's history. Our deepest thanks also go to Rémi Baudin, vice chairman of the Board of Directors, Bernard Carton,

CFO from 1975 to 2000, and Pierre Bellon's family members.

In addition, we would like to thank historians Jacques Marseille and Catherine Hodeir for their audit of the group's history and for carrying out a large number of interviews.

Our thanks also go to Emily Borgeaud, whose alert and enthusiastic quill brought Sodexho's culture and history to life.

Finally, we would especially like to thank the internal team comprising Clodine Pincemin, Isabelle Honoré, Marion Cavoué, Nathalie Da Costa and William Mengebier of the Group's Communications and Sustainable Development department for their endless dedication over many months. Steve Brady, senior vice president, Communications, North America, and Phil Hooper, director of Corporate Affairs and Communications, UK and Ireland, have also been of great help with the English version.

This book reflects the contributions and work of more than 110 individuals, a small number compared to all of the players in the Sodexho adventure – and the story of Sodexho is far from over.

Index

Photo Credits

14   Old port of Marseilles: Marseilles municipal archives. EM art. 10 no. 206.

15   Compagnie Mixte poster: http://www.theshipslist.com/ships/lines/mixte.htm.

17   Pierre Bellon: Édouard Richard.

20   Le Soudanais: Service Historique de la Défense, Maritime department, Vincennes. D11 no. 1.

38   Jacques Tavel: personal archives. Pierre Sannini: personal archives.

44   André Langlois: personal archives.

62   Marie-Pierre Le Lohé: Daniel Gaugez.

83   Giacomo Sorlini: Daniel Gaugez.

98   Desert: George Beyrouti.

100   Anne-Marie Maisonnave: personal archives.

107   Jean-Michel Dhenain: Daniel Gaugez.

118   Pierre Henry: Steve Murez.

130   Clodine Pincemin: Steve Murez.

163   Garry C. Knox: Philippe Couette.

164   Michel Landel: Philippe Couette.

184   Paul Bonnette: Daniel Gaugez.

188   Laurent Cousin: Michel Labelle.

198   Philippe Voraz: Michel Labelle.

201   Elisabeth Carpentier: Michel Labelle.

208   "Welcome, Mister John": Procitel.

208   Stand (Tour de France 1993): Bruno Bade. Bicycle (Village Sodexho, Dinan, Tour de France 1995): J.Y. Ruszniewski (Agence Temp Sport).

232   George Chavel: Steve Murez.

236   Siân Herbert-Jones: Steve Murez.

239   Patrick Poireau: Steve Murez.

260   Elisabeth Carpentier: Michel Labelle.

269   Yann Coléou: Steve Murez.

270   Philippe Taillet: Steve Murez.

272   Siân Herbert-Jones: Steve Murez.

276   Nicolas Japy: Michel Labelle.

280   Philip Jansen: Michel Labelle.

281   Richard Macedonia: Michel Labelle.

281   Sophie Clamens: Éric Avenel.

282   Rick Brockland: Michel Labelle.

290   Jacques Pétry: Philippe Brazil.

292   Michel Landel: Michel Labelle.

Cover photo: Sylvain Ageorges.
All other photos from the Sodexho Group Media Library.

Translated by Alison Kim and Gordon Golding (ICC)
Editing: Elizabeth Mac Callum
Printing coordination: Marie-Hélène Sicard, Marketing, Sodexho Canada
Typesetting by Infoscan Collette, Quebec
Colophon: Marquis Book Printing
Copyright: October, 2006
Printed in Canada